HISTORY HUNTERS

Chandragupta Vikramaditya and the Shaka Conspiracy

Shruti Garodia is an incurable reader and writer, with an abiding passion for history. She loves bringing alive the past for children through storytelling. She is the co-author of *The History of India for Children* (Hachette India, 2018), a bestselling two-volume set. Shruti graduated from Cornell University, USA, and holds degrees in engineering and finance. She has lived in New York and London during her career in banking. A keen traveller, she loves to explore historic sites and museums, and enjoys trying new adventures like scuba diving, trekking and sailing.

Archana Garodia Gupta is the co-author of the bestselling *The History of India for Children*, and the author of *The Women Who Ruled India* (Hachette India, 2019). With a lifelong passion for books, languages, travel and history, she has a knack for weaving delightful nuggets of information into engaging tales. A leading national quizzer, she has won the 'Champion of Champions' title from BBC's *Mastermind India* and is regularly seen on national TV as an expert on the immensely popular show, *Kaun Banega Crorepati*. She was the national president of FICCI Ladies Organization. She holds an MBA from IIM-Ahmedabad and is the founder of Touchstone, a digital-first jewellery brand.

OTHER BOOKS IN THE SERIES

HISTORY HUNTERS 1

Chandragupta Maurya and the Greek Onslaught

HISTORY HUNTERS 2

Akbar and the Agents from the East

HISTORY HUNTERS

Chandragupta Vikramaditya and the Shaka Conspiracy

Shruti Garodia
Archana Garodia Gupta

Illustrations by Priya Kuriyan

First published in 2023 by Hachette India
(Registered name: Hachette Book Publishing India Pvt. Ltd)
An Hachette UK company
www.hachetteindia.com

SRD

ISBN 978-93-93701-95-4

Hachette Book Publishing India Pvt. Ltd
4th & 5th Floors, Corporate Centre
Plot No. 94, Sector 44, Gurugram – 122003, India

Typeset by Manmohan Kumar, Delhi

Printed and bound in India
by Manipal Technologies Limited

MEET THE

ZOYA ALI (12 years): A book lover with a passion for learning about anything and everything…and sharing her knowledge, whether her friends want it or not. Her natural indolence is often overcome by her insatiable curiosity, which leads her into adventures.

EKNOOR SINGH (12 years): Zoya's outspoken best friend and comrade-in-arms. This fearless warrior is always willing to take on anyone, anytime, and is invariably the first to rush into the unknown.

ANSH DESAI (11 years): The youngest of the group, who is usually dragged reluctantly into various escapades. This loyal youngster is always on the lookout for tasty treats as a reaction to his mother's many health fads.

ROHAN MATHAI (13 years): A nature lover with an uncanny ability to make even wild animals trust him. This quiet, level-headed teenager can always be counted upon.

ELFU (13 years): a mischievous young elephant who believes he's human – especially when it comes to food. Rohan's constant companion since childhood, Elfu depends on his 'big brother' to protect him, undeterred by their size difference.

WHAT HAPPENED BEFORE THIS…

In History Hunters 1: Chandragupta Maurya and the Greek Onslaught, *four friends – Zoya, Eknoor, Ansh and Rohan – are thrown back two millennia through time and space into Mauryan times, right in the middle of a battle between Alexander of Macedonia and the Indian king Puru (Porus). A young man comes to their rescue, but the foursome have to deal with a slew of hazards before they can get back home.*

In History Hunters 2: Akbar and the Agents from the East, *the foursome's time-travelling adventure lands them in the court of the Mughal emperor Akbar. What with having to dodge poisoned cloaks, overcome fierce warriors and even escape execution by elephant, Zoya, Eknoor, Ansh and Rohan have to use all their wits and all their resources to accomplish their mission and get back home.*

Now, another challenge is coming their way, and they have no clue what it is…

Noor stretched luxuriously – summer vacation was here! No school to go to early in the morning and no annoying history–geography! *Hmm...I wonder when my kung fu camp is supposed to start. And we are going to Amritsar to meet Nani–Nana next week! Kulchas. Yum. I wonder if Mummy will let me do the Ginormous Paratha Challenge.* Just the thought made her salivate.

Thunderous knocking interrupted the 12-year old's delicious daydream. *Uff...who was it?* She knew it had to be one of her three friends who lived in the Miracle of the Forest Eco-Resort in Goa with her, along with their parents who worked there.

'Let me in! Open! Quick!' a boy's voice came through urgently. She rolled her eyes. 'Argh! Ansh! It's so early.'

'Pleaaase let me in! My mum is after me!'

Noor immediately got up and opened the front door. Though Ansh and she loved to bug each other, they presented a united front before Parental Forces.

Her nose wrinkled as she ushered her friend in. 'God, Ansh, why are you smelling like a herb factory?'

The 11-year-old burst out, 'Ma keeps wanting to put lavender oil on me to heal my "emotional distress"! I keep telling her my emotions are just fine...but then she keeps asking why I "escape" to the waterfall every weekend?'

He continued, 'And then, what can I possibly tell her? I can hardly say that there's a portal there, and my friends and I keep time-travelling and meeting great emperors like Chandragupta Maurya and Akbar!' Ansh had a wild, slightly hunted look in his eyes.

Noor nodded along understandingly. 'Yes...Priya Aunty *is* out there, but this will be too much even for *her* imagination...'

Noor, Ansh and their friends Zoya and Rohan – and Rohan's pet elephant Elfu – had been having some insane adventures, which sounded like they were right out of a sci-fi TV show. A few weeks ago, they had somehow been flung back 2,500 years in the past and landed up on the battlefield where Alexander the Greek had been fighting King Porus! After braving many hazards and perils, they had managed to return home, only to end up in the Mughal emperor Akbar's court a few days later. It sounded too outlandish to admit out loud.

Noor got up with a bounce. 'Okay, come, let's slip off to the Salsette Nature Reserve. No Ansh, No Problem!' They found Zoya and Rohan in the garden next door, whispering furiously to each other, and hustled them along.

Zoya was saying, 'Just got a text from Sid Lal *again*. He wants to meet us! I've already been ignoring him for the past two weeks!' Sid Lal was the tech gazillionaire who had developed The Portal, the time machine that had been sending them off on their recent exploits.

Rohan looked upset. 'I'm *realllly* not sure about this, Zo,' he said. 'We don't know why he's doing this…and what if the parentals find out? We'll be grounded. Forever.'

'Or worse!' Ansh added. 'Ma will take away my phone… she hates those things anyway.' He shuddered dramatically.

Zoya looked unhappy but said, 'Hmm, we're decided then. No going back in time or meeting Sid Lal until further notice.' Noor looked as disappointed. She did love going on adventures…and these were the best! But she kept quiet.

They had almost reached Ansh's cottage in the row of staff houses. 'Guys! Watch it!' Ansh said in an urgent whisper. As they crouched and tiptoed beneath the front window, they gave each other congratulatory looks. They were almost past the danger zone.

Or not.

'Ohhhh, childrennnnn…there you are,' wafted out the dulcet tones of Nirvana, the resident detox/spiritual/yoga Chief Wellness Officer of the Miracle in the Forest Eco-resort. AKA…Ansh's Ma.

They stopped dead in their tracks. Uh-oh.

All four turned around to face her. 'Ye-e-e-s, Priya Aunty?' asked Zoya with an innocent air.

The lady, wearing a sleek bodysuit, with a turban wrapped around her hair, said abstractedly, 'How often do I have to say that I shall be known only as Nirvana henceforth…

'Okay, kiddos, please come along…just need you for *one* teeny-tiny experiment…' She smiled sweetly, and made her eyes big and imploring. That look never failed to get everyone around Priya, sorry, Nirvana, to do what she wanted...no matter how reluctantly.

She started leading them a little distance away. 'Where is she taking us?' whispered Noor frustratedly. She disliked Nirvana Aunty's flights of fancy the most.

'Dunno,' replied Zoya with a shrug. 'Looks like the new ultra-fancy holistic centre that is...the spa...that Dad is developing with her!' Zoya's father was the general manager of the resort, and was making it a go-to spot for Goa ecotourism. Ansh was looking glummer and glummer. He knew better than anyone what unusual torments his mom could conjure up.

As they reached the spa building, Ansh's mom turned to them with a big, excited smile. 'So! I want to make sure our guests have the most extraordinary healing experience here. And the first step to making sure *you* glow is to make your skin glow! I had the best idea...just need a few human trials...'

Okay. This they could deal with. Some sort of body scrub...*wait! Human trials?*

'*Ta-da*! Here is it! WRIGGLE NIBBLES – the world's first worm spa!' She beamed beatifically at all of them as she pointed down at a giant bathtub.

Ansh and the others looked down in utter horror.

The tub was full of wriggly white maggots!

'These are special indigenous maggots harvested from the south of Maharashtra – they nibble away all your dead skin...and your negative emotions too!'

They turned around to face her s-l-o-w-l-y like zombies. Was she *serious*? She continued obliviously, 'So you just climb in gently, and let them *washhh* over you... So, who is going to volunteer? Rohan? You? I know you love animals! This will be a beautiful way to *commmmunnnne* with some of our precious planet's smaller creatures.' She gave Rohan an encouraging pat.

With a jolt, Rohan came out of his trance. What was Nirvana Aunty saying? *Eeurgh.* He was not about to step into this appalling mass of slithering sliminess! He shuddered. Sensing Rohan's disgust, Nirvana turned and said, 'Noor? I know you're always up for an adventure...'

The children looked around desperately for a way to escape this nightmare they had found themselves in. As Nirvana came to pat Zoya encouragingly on her shoulder, the 12-year-old pulled away and ran out of the room, calling back, 'Just a minute, Aunty, w-a-i-t.'

She tore out of the building blindly and came to a gasping stop. *Gross.* Feeling a little sick, she bent over, face down, hands on her thighs – and gradually realized that she was staring down at a pair of extremely shiny and rather large black leather shoes. She slowly straightened and her eyes travelled up a buff, muscled figure dressed in a business suit.

Uh-oh. Sid Lal's bodyguard! From the frying pan into the fire!

He said in a deep, rumbly voice, 'Good morning, Ms Ali – Mr Lal has been trying to get in touch...for A WHILE.'

Zoya gave the man a nervous sideways look. Sid Lal, though her father's childhood friend, was a multi-billionaire and extremely powerful. Not used to being crossed.

The bulky bodyguard continued to stare at her impassively and silently. She stuttered, 'Yes, yes, we were *just* about to drop in…right now, actually…Rohan! Noor! Ansh! Come, *fast*.' – the last in a semi-shout.

They appeared so quickly, it was clear they'd been looking for any way to escape from their writhing white nightmare. Ansh's mother was hard on their heels, a little frown on her forehead.

Zoya widened her eyes and said, 'Guys! Remember we had that appointment with Mr Lal to discuss…uh…those internships with him? We must go NOW.'

Rohan gave Zoya a look, mouthing silently, 'WHAT! We had decided NO.' She indicated the bodyguard with her eyes and shrugged helplessly.

Nirvana Aunty stepped in, protesting, 'No, no, you can't go yet. Just one quick dip in the worm pool…'

Urgh! At the mention of the wriggly horror movie inside, Noor and Ansh chimed in at the same time, 'Yes, Zoya, let's go NOW. Mustn't be late.'

Zoya put on her most persuasive face. 'Aunty, I mean Nirvana, it is Very, Very Important that we go. Career Prospects and Growing Up and all. Look! Mr Lal has even sent an escort to fetch us.' The foursome went up to the intimidating bodyguard, and tried smiling brightly as he glowered down at them menacingly.

•••••••••••••••

As they walked along towards the driveway of the resort, the bodyguard rumbled, 'Let's not forget the little elephant. Mr Lal told me to make sure.' Rohan and Ansh gave each other apprehensive looks. Sid Lal was only interested in Elfu when he wanted to send them all back in time. This was NOT a good idea. What DID He Want?

Noor saw their expressions and hissed at them, 'Two words. Worm. Spa.' Rohan recoiled and began marching swiftly towards the shed where Elfu was kept.

Elfu let out a loud, happy harrumph as he smelt his human pals approaching. He jiggled his ears excitedly and kept rubbing his trunk over the children's heads.

As the children walked silently from the resort to the neighbouring estate, their apprehension grew. Zoya quietly raised an eyebrow to the others, indicating the steady flow of people driving and motorbiking up the driveway towards Sid Lal's long Portuguese-style mansion.

Oblivious to the tense undercurrents, Elfu was just happy to be out and about, wandering around with his buddies. Though this particular human in the front did scare him a bit. *What was that dark thing on his face?* Elfu started imagining how he would look with fancy sunglasses. *Hmm.* As his trunk snaked out to pluck the intriguing toy from the human's face, 'We are here,' rumbled Elfu's almost-victim.

They all came to a stop.

There stood Sid Lal. And he did not look happy.

• • • • • • • • • • • • • • •

Sid Lal stared at the children coldly for a full minute without saying anything. As sweat began to bead Rohan's brow, Sid Lal finally said, 'Hello. Well, if it isn't my favourite children.'

They all gulped. Even Elfu.

'Hello, Mr Lal,' muttered Zoya nervously. 'Actually. Hmm. We had exams, you know…'

'Sid…please do call me Sid,' he broke in. An uneasy silence descended, Sid Lal looking at the youngsters consideringly, Zoya trying to say what had to be said.

Rohan decided to bite the bullet. 'So actually…Mr Lal, we are not sure about going in The Po…'

Sid Lal interrupted once more. 'Children!' he said in a tone that brooked no opposition. 'There is something you must see! Come, follow me. Get the elephant.'

He came down the steps and led the little group around the side of the vast mansion.

'Now, where are we going?' hissed Noor to Zoya. 'It's always dangerous when an adult starts leading us into unknown buildings!'

Zoya shrugged. 'Dunno. Let's see…'

On the side of the mansion was a large open area that looked sort of like a...parking lot? Dozens of cars and bikes were standing in neat rows. From there a wide path led off into dense foliage.

The group followed Sid Lal a little uncertainly. After walking through a long stretch of forest, the path led to a clearing on the other side.

A plain white one-storeyed building stood in front of them. The centre section had a very large, panelled glass door with a semicircular top – in the Portuguese style as well. Smaller matching windows flanked it.

'Come, come,' said Sid Lal.

'What about Elfu?' asked Rohan uncertainly.

'Yes, bring him along too.'

Okkkkayy. The children exchanged looks.

Elfu just about managed to fit through the large door. They walked in a little way and stopped. And just stared.

'What IS this?' whispered Ansh.

It felt like they had suddenly gone from 18th-century Portugal to the 25th century!

They were standing on a platform of some sort. Instead of tracks, there was what looked like a large, round metallic tube, but with a flat bottom. Glowing circles spanned the diameter at intervals.

Sid Lal watched their stunned expressions with a small smile. He said, 'Presenting...the Hyperloop!'

'The Hyperloop?'

He replied, 'Yes. An ultra-high-speed train that runs on magnets. We have topped 500 kilometres an hour so far. The idea is to reach 1,250 kilometres per hour...'

'But where does it go???' exclaimed Noor excitedly. 'Can we goooo on it?'

'Well, for this trial, I decided to run a line between my home and The Portal!' Sid Lal said. 'Didn't you wonder where all those people in the cave-office came from? The entrance you found was used by us only in the beginning. This is far more efficient.'

Zoya burst out, 'I thought there was no functioning Hyperloop yet! Many people around the world have been working on this for decades. How come no one KNOWS about it...this is HUGE news!'

Sid Lal said enigmatically, 'My employees know how to keep things quiet...if they know what's good for them...'

A capsule drew up silently. It was a sleek, bullet-shaped cylinder that fit into the large tube. They all looked on fascinated as the doors opened automatically. Inside it were two moulded seats of hard plastic, with seat belts that strapped in each person securely across the chest and legs.

'So, what do you say? Do you want to have a try?'

Noor immediately said, 'YES, YES!' The others looked on, excited but cautious.

'Oh! What about Elfu??' said Rohan worriedly.

Sid Lal answered, 'Not to worry.' He whispered to his bodyguard, who disappeared into the operator's office. Soon, another – larger – capsule arrived from the other side and magnetically attached itself to the previous one at the platform.

'Come, little elephant,' Sid Lal said, leading the way. This bigger capsule was empty, except for plenty of harnesses. This capsule was clearly meant for luggage or cargo.

Rohan soothed Elfu as he was secured with various harnesses. 'Don't worry, Elfu-baba…this is going to be fun. You love adventures, right?'

'Rohan, you – and one more person – had better go on the first ride so you can offload the elephant,' commanded Sid Lal.

Rohan and Noor went and strapped in, eager and apprehensive.

'Don't worry, children. It will be only 40 seconds. You'll feel pressure as the speed increases and your ears may pop…but it will be quick!'

The doors closed smoothly. And with a whoosh, they were off! The speed increased incredibly swiftly. Rohan and Noor held onto the side handles. Just as it felt like it was going way too fast, the capsule decelerated and came to a smooth stop.

They kept sitting for a minute or so. Then, Noor gingerly unlatched her harness. 'Hunh. That felt…weird. Very weird.'

They doddered to the gate and pressed the button to open it. People were waiting to receive them.

Rohan rushed to the other capsule, to check on his Elfu, muttering, 'I'm sure he will be anxious after this strange experience…poor baby.'

But the doors parted to reveal an extremely pleased-looking Elfu. *What a ride! Let's go again!*

As the children waited on the platform with the merry young pachyderm, chatting about their superfast journey, the others showed up in two more capsules.

Zoya's eyes were shining. She did love trying new things...especially when it was before others!

•••••••••••••••

After they had all entered the cave-office, Sid Lal turned to them. 'So, what do you think?'

'Amah-zing! So fun!' said Noor. 'I'm ready to go again!'

'In a while,' said the billionaire. 'For now, I want you to go to the Gupta period. We've had a signal showing a high probability of meeting Emperor Chandragupta Vikramaditya.'

Zoya burst out indignantly, 'The Gupta period? I've been researching all about the Cholas!' As the other children turned incredulous faces to her, she caught herself. 'Err, just to be prepared – like the Girl Scouts, you know...' she trailed off feebly. *Oops. Maybe she had said too much.* Zoya had started getting addicted to these little adventures. She had convinced herself there was no *real* danger.

Ansh muttered darkly, 'I always knew I was on to something when I came up with your nickname, "Zany Zoya"!'

Rohan spoke up quietly but determinedly, 'Look, sir, we are not sure that all this travelling back in time is a good idea. At all. What if we get stuck back there? What if something happens to Elfu? We're hiding this from our parents...'

The others nodded, Ansh emphatically, and Noor and Zoya more reluctantly.

Sid Lal looked at them silently for a moment. 'You know, children,' he said coldly, 'I am giving you The. Chance. Of. A. Lifetime. How many others get the opportunity to save the world and be a part of something so big? We need those DNA strands from the great people of the past to isolate the gene for greatness. I will do this. With or without you. If you are not up to the task, it's okay. I will figure out a way. With others more willing...'

He turned away dismissively, beckoning his bodyguard over. 'He will take you back now.'

'No, no! Wait,' Zoya burst out desperately. 'That's not what we meant.' They had doubts about this whole thing, but they weren't ready for it to be snatched away in an instant!

'Look, I am a busy person. Choose.' Sid Lal added, a little more cajolingly, 'I will be happy to have you on board. But you must decide one way or the other.'

As he saw the four children looking at each other, he waited impassively.

After some unspoken communication, Zoya stepped forward and said, her voice wavering a bit, 'Okay... we're in.'

'Well, so it's decided then. No more of this. The choice is yours.' He stared at them, willing them to agree with him.

'Err, yes. Yes.' They nodded to one another.

'There's no time to lose, then. You must go immediately to Magadha...its capital Pataliputra, to be precise! Remember, find Chandragupta Vikramaditya, get one strand of hair, and come straight back. Don't hang around.'

Ansh said, 'Where is Magadha? It sounds vaguely familiar...'

Zoya stopped and stared at Ansh in proper horror. 'Ansh. Desai!!! Magadha? You know, Magadha? In the east? Most important region in India for a thousand years?'

As he looked blank, she rolled her eyes and said, 'Ancient Bihar, Ansh! We have to go to Patna!'

He just rolled his eyes back at her and smirked.

Noor, meanwhile, turned to Sid Lal and said fiercely. 'Listen here, mister. I refuse to keep pretending to be a boy every time. Enough is enough!'

He gave her an intense stare. *Oops!* thought Noor. *Maybe I pushed it too much.* 'Fine.' he said. He went and started tinkering with the big, glowing screen.

'Oh, and don't forget to give us some money this time...life is quite hard when we land up in a strange place and don't have a rupee to share between us.' Noor added cheekily with a smile.

Zoya interjected, 'Err, actually in Gupta times it was not the rupee...' Noor gave Zoya a look.

Sid Lal gazed at them impatiently and said, 'Yes, yes, I have changed the settings. Now, go.'

The four children stood in front of the screen, all holding on to Elfu.

Sid Lal pressed a button and off they went, clutching one another and trying to keep their balance as the world began to spin crazily around them and the noise increased to a roar.

•••••••••••••••

Once the world was still, they opened their eyes. Elfu reluctantly detached his trunk from Rohan's waist, which he had clutched a little too tightly. Rohan took a deep breath in relief. An overwhelming smell of floral and sandalwood perfumes, and a cacophony of sounds assailed him simultaneously.

He looked around. They seemed to be in some sort of busy marketplace with shops lining the square on all sides. Crowds of shoppers strolled past stalls of all sorts – piled with fruits and vegetables. To one side, goldsmiths were sitting and fashioning gold and precious stones into elaborate jewellery, while nearby, metalworkers hammered out copper vessels with loud thwangs. Other stalls had blossoms and buds piled up, with garlands and flower jewellery in intricate designs.

Vendors were crying out, hawking their wares, while shoppers were engaged in friendly bargaining here and there. Rich ladies were being carried around at a leisurely pace in palanquins held by eight to ten bearers each.

Both men and women were mostly dressed in cotton clothes – dhotis of some sort – wrapped tight or loose, long or short – wait, some were even in sarongs?! Everyone had long, flowing scarves...some had them hanging from their necks down the front, some the other way around. A few were using the long cloths to cover their heads. Some women were wearing bandeau-style blouses. And the colours! All the clothes around them seemed to be in all the hues of the rainbow...and so many different prints... *bandhani*, block, *ikat*...!

'Look, Zo! Why are people dressed so differently from one another?' Noor asked Zoya.

'Hmm.' Zoya looking around. 'See,' she pointed out, 'the poorer folk are in just loincloths. Those fancily dressed men must be noblemen...is that an umbrella??'

They turned to look at a couple of young men and a lady dressed in fancy silk dhotis and scarves. They had attendants carrying some kind of umbrellas over them, made of what seemed like large, dried leaves! The people under them were laden with fragrant floral jewellery – garlands, bracelets, anklets – with flowers woven even into their long, curly hair...and with gold and gemstones as well. The lady had her hair up in an elaborate knot and a large lotus was tucked into it.

In fact, all the people around, from peasant to prince, all looked like walking-talking gardens! Both men and women had flowers wrapped around their hair, neck, wrists, waist...

'Look at those groups of Jain *munis*!' exclaimed Ansh. 'I saw so many when I visited Mount Abu...how do they survive without clothes!' He added, 'And those are Buddhists,' pointing out shaven-headed monks with downcast eyes, wearing robes of maroon and yellow, and carrying begging bowls. 'And see, a sadhu! He has covered himself in ash!' He indicated a man with long dreadlocks, wearing a loincloth and smeared all over in a white powdery substance. Ansh's mother was always exploring different religions, and it was showing.

Noor exclaimed again. 'Check out the hairrrr. Insannne!' They all looked around, noticing the hairstyles. 'Those must have taken hoursss to do,' exclaimed Zoya, noting the loops and curls and knots studded with jewels and nets of pearls. Many men and women wore bands on their heads with pearls suspended from them; many others wore fine muslin turbans.

Jewels gleamed on every conceivable and inconceivable part of the human body – hair, *kundala*s in the ear, necklaces of all lengths, golden snakes coiled on the upper arm, bangles, bracelets and rings, waistbands, hip bands, upper-thigh bands, anklets – you name it!

Rohan was excited. 'Guys! Look! How many pets do these guys keep?' pointing to a large variety of pet shops. There were men selling monkeys, birds, puppies…were those mongooses?

It was all so overwhelming.

• • • • • • • • • • • • • • • •

'At least we are girls this time,' muttered Zoya, looking down and then at the others. She and Noor were wearing embroidered dhotis of delicate muslin with bandeaus on top, and a long scarf hanging down their necks. She checked her head with her hand. She had such an elaborate hairdo! The boys were wearing white dhotis with woven borders, and gold double-chains crossing across their chests.

'We should try and fit in,' Noor said in one of her typical super-loud whispers. 'Look! We need to go get some of this art on our faces...' She had adored face paint at birthday parties when she was little...in fact, she still loved it, but secretly. Almost-teens were meant to have grown out of such childish things.

Zoya piped in, 'Yes, and some of this flower jewellery as well...smells soooo good.'

She checked the pouch at her waist and saw with satisfaction that there were coins in there, in copper, bronze, silver – and even a gorgeous gold one!

They wandered over to a stall laden with flowers of all sorts. The shopkeeper was a simply dressed woman with completely white hair, a mass of wrinkles and old, kindly eyes.

'Young ladies and gents, come and adorn yourselves,' she said a pleasant voice.

They realized that they could understand this language. 'This isn't Sanskrit!' muttered Ansh. 'Zo! What did people speak in this time?? And actually, WHEN is this time?'

'Ansh! I dunno...we are probably sometime in the fourth century.'

'Aah. BCE?' asked Ansh.

'NO!' Zoya replied, completely exasperated. 'CE. CE!' She continued, 'You are right. This isn't Sanskrit. Hmm. Must be a Prakrit of some sort.'

Ansh breathed in the beautiful scents deeply. 'It reminds me of when we used to go to the temple in Mumbai,' he murmured. Zoya and Noor began sifting through the different types of flower jewellery eagerly.

After trying on various combinations, the girls chose yellow and white garlands, fragrant *kadamba* flowers for their hair, and flower bracelets and wristbands.

'A little bit of face paint and we should be good,' nudged Noor. They wandered over to a shop close by. It looked like an art supply shop…but the only painting going on was on people's faces and bodies! The artist came up with a smile to Rohan, who immediately backed away, 'Not for me, please!'

The artist shrugged and painted a simple tilak of sandalwood paste on Rohan's forehead. 'Okay,' sighed the teen with relief, 'This I can live with.'

Zoya went up. The woman asked her, 'Basic or custom?'

'Basic, please.'

'A'ight. Whatever the young lady wants. Flower, leaf or animal pattern?'

'Erm. Flower, please.' Zoya tried to stay still as the artist began painting sandalwood and white paste patterns delicately on her cheeks.

Elfu knocked on Rohan's shoulder with his trunk. As his human brother looked up, he used his trunk to point to the artist finishing up Zoya's face with a flourish.

'Yes, Elfu, just hang on.'

'Wow! I love this…' exclaimed Zoya, as she admired herself, gazing into a highly polished brass mirror with an elaborate back. Noor was next. She sat down and said eagerly, 'Animals, please, for me, ma'am!' waiting for the artist to start on her face.

As she carefully began to paint Noor's face in a motif of peacocks, monkeys, birds and even a small elephant, Elfu began feeling more and more indignant. Why should the others have all the fun? He also wanted some face paint. They *knew* he loved dressing up, didn't they? Besides, it reminded him of his childhood in Kerala when his mum would have patterns drawn lovingly on her face before a temple ceremony. Maybe he could get a garland too...he nudged Rohan with his trunk again and let out a small harrumph.

When Rohan just stroked his trunk absent-mindedly, continuing to look around him, Elfu decided to make his feelings rather clearer. He extended his trunk and delicately plucked the peacock-feather-backed paintbrush with which the artist was painting patterns onto Noor's face.

'Whattt the heck!' exclaimed Noor, startled.

The artist shouted, 'See what your *gaja* is doing!' Everyone looked up and saw that Elfu had inverted his trunk and was trying to paint his own forehead!

After a stunned silence, the entire group dissolved into snorts of laughter. 'Oh, Elfu!' gasped Zoya, her eyes watering as she spluttered hysterically. 'You look like you're painting your own Jackson Pollock!'

'Jacksowhoo?' Rohan said, turning to Zoya.

'Oh, you don't know about Jackson Pollock? It's *really interesting*, actually. He was a famous American artist... lots of abstract stuff where he dripped the paint anyh...' She broke off as she saw them rolling their eyes. Zo was in The Zone again! 'Honestly, guys, with you...' She laughed reluctantly and trailed off.

Elfu, meanwhile, was pursuing his new-found hobby with abandon, creating what could only be described as sandalwood-paste graffiti on his forehead.

Rohan, who was well used to Elfu's antics, went up to the elephant and said with a smile, 'Fine, Elfu-baba, we'll get your face painted too.' The local face-paint artist's eyes were popping out at this spectacle. She said faintly, 'Yes, yes, there is a place close by that does elephant decorations too. Just a few shops along on the right.'

'Oi!' said a loud, high voice. 'What on earth is your elephant doing?!' It was in the same Prakrit language as spoken by the shopkeeper and the artist.

They turned around and saw a dark-skinned girl about their own age, holding a little boy, about three years old, by his hand. She was dressed very finely, in a brocade silk dhoti and bandeau blouse that glistened in the sunshine. She was slim and athletic, with a long, fancy-looking pearl, ruby, emerald and sapphire necklace looped around her neck, and gold ornaments sprinkled about her.

Her hair was knotted in a complicated bun, but wisps had escaped to frame her face in a halo, and she somehow looked bedraggled despite all her finery.

'Oh, blast it! This *uttariya* is always fluttering and getting in my way!' She exclaimed. She set her teeth and draped her long *chunni*-type scarf across her right shoulder, tying it firmly on the other side at the waist. 'There, that should do it.'

The little boy with her was looking around curiously, one thumb in his mouth. He too was dressed in a yellow silk dhoti, with black kajal in his eyes, a gold belt around his waist and tinkling gold anklets.

'Oh my god! These two look like they have escaped from the local Krishna Leela!' exclaimed Ansh in a loud whisper. Noor grinned in response. At the unfamiliar sound of English, the girl's eyes narrowed suspiciously, but before she could say anything, the little boy said imperiously, 'Paba! Pabaaa!'

She looked down at him and then looked up at the rest of them. 'My little brother. He's a pain! He insisted on coming along with me, so I *had* to bring him…they would have caught me otherwise…' The girl trailed off mysteriously, rolling her eyes before looking around as if watching for someone.

'Hello, what is your name?' said Rohan gently in Prakrit, bending down to the toddler.

'Kuma-guta!' lisped the little boy.

'Koo-ma gut-ta?' exclaimed Zoya interestedly. *That sounded Japanese! Not usual for this region of Bihar.*

'No! Not Kooma-gutta. Yuv-waj Kuma-guta! I'm da pwince!' The little boy became frustrated at this mispronunciation of his lordly name.

The children looked at each other, baffled. As the toddler stamped his small foot angrily, the girl interjected, 'It is Kumaragupta! His name is bigger than he is!' She gave him a half-affectionate, half-exasperated look and tousled his hair. She continued, a little self-importantly 'And I am Prabhavati Gupta, royal princess of Magadha...and all of the immense Gupta Empire.'

Oooh. Zoya's eyes widened as she started to connect the dots. *What a random piece of luck. She was the daughter of the man they had to get a strand of hair from – Emperor Chandragupta Vikramaditya himself! And ohmigod, was this the future emperor Kumaragupta?*

She smiled at the teenage girl, who continued, 'Argh! There's this huge Vasantotsav party that I'm supposed to be getting all dolled up for. But I really, really, badly wanted to see the horse-riding show that's on in the *maidan*. The Shaka troupe is in town! I've heard they can do the most amazing things on horseback. My stepmother spotted me leaving and wouldn't hear of it.' She put on a simpering voice 'It's not *lady*like, Prabha...you're a *groooown* woman now!'

At this last bit, Noor choked out, 'Wait, just how old are you?'

'I'm thirteen,' replied the other girl. She continued huffily, 'If it was up to *her*, she'd make Daddy stop all my fun lessons like horse riding and weapons trai...'

'Wait, that's my practically my age! How does that make you a grown woman?!' broke in Noor incredulously.

Prabhavati looked at her impatiently. 'Why, the party is to celebrate *my* engagement! My wedding will be in three months! My fiancé and his family have come over all the way from the west…Vidarbha. He seemed nice enough when I sneaked a peek from the palace balcony, though pale-ish…' She trailed off.

Noor's eyes widened. *It was normal to get married at 13 in these times? To be considered a grown-up?*

'Wait a minute. How old is your fiancé?' she exclaimed.

'Ohh, I don't know. Must be 16 or 17 –' the other girl replied breezily. Her eyes narrowed. 'Wait, why is this such a surprise to you…and what was that language that boy was speaking? You're not from around here! Where are you from?!' She glared at them suspiciously.

Oops! Five minutes in a new place and they were already in hot water! Rohan thought for a second and said, 'We are from very far away. From the north, you know. Kashmir… the land of lakes and mountains.'

The princess's eyes widened. 'Oh, Kashmir! That's one kingdom Daddy hasn't gotten around to conquering yet… maybe next year…' she ended with a smirk. At this, Ansh poked Noor in her side, and they gave each other silent laughing looks. She was quite full of herself, this one!

Prabhavati added with gracious condescension, 'You are welcome to my land…but what are you doing here?'

As always, when stuck in a tight spot, Zoya was struck by inspiration. 'We are a musical troupe, my sister and brothers and I. We've journeyed all the way to Magadha to learn the special veena-playing techniques developed by Samrat Samudragupta.'

'My grandfather...' whispered Prabhavati reverently. 'He was something else...what a conqueror. And you should have seen him on a horse...oh! The horse show! We must go!'

Ansh sniggered internally. *Princess PG seemed quite horse-mad! More concerned about missing this horse show than her own engagement party!*

The princess's one-track mind was back on its track. Horse track, that is. 'ANYway, I really want to see this Shaka horse performance. But even Daddy put his foot down this time.' She pouted. 'He said it wouldn't look good for the royal princess to mingle with the Shakas when relations are so tense...especially when she is getting married to a Vakataka prince.'

The others were looking more and more mystified, but Zoya was nodding along knowingly as the princess rambled on.

'The Waka-whos? Shaka-Shakira? What is she going on about?' muttered Ansh in English. 'Is this ancient India or a pop concert?'

'Did you never study about the Guptas? Honestly, Ansh, I don't know what you do during history class!' whispered Zoya to him from the side of her mouth.

'I ignore it like most kids, Zany Zo!' he replied, sticking his tongue out slightly.

Prabhavati was winding up her rant '...so ANYway, I decided to give the palace guards the slip and just crept away. *This* little brat saw me and came running to join me, so I had to get him with me…I have very little time, but now I can't find where the show is being held!' She sighed glumly.

'Hey!' – she perked up – 'Why don't you all come with me as well? These guys can do crazy things – like shooting insanely accurate arrows at a full gallop. You'd never have seen anything like it!'

Noor was instantly up for the idea. She loved anything to do with sports – the more dangerous, the better!

'Heyyy, ya…let's go, guys.' She saw Ansh's dubious expression and glared at him.

Zoya jumped in. 'Let's go with her… We need to find a way to meet her father…you know…Chandragupta Vikramaditya?!' she whispered in English, with a knowing wiggle of her eyebrows.

Noor got very excited. 'Chanduuu! I want to meet Chandu again.' Her thoughts flashed back to a couple of weeks ago, when they had spent a day with a teenage Chandragupta Maurya in Takshashila. 'But wait. You said we are in some CE century?' She started looking confused.

Zoya hissed 'Uffo, Noor! Not Chandragupta Maurya… not *our* Chandu. Chandragupta Vikramaditya-Chandu!' At Noor's uncomprehending expression, she said, 'Uhh, magnificent Gupta emperor Chandu?'

'Why would two of the most famous kings of India both be called Chandragupta?' whined Noor in annoyance. 'What's a poor student like me to do?'

Zoya rolled her eyes. 'I'll explain later. Just come. We'll call this one Vik for short. And FYI, we are in the fourth century CE – 700 years after "our" Chandu!'

Elfu was looking back at the painter's shop mournfully, but Rohan grabbed his trunk and tugged him along, saying, 'Yes, yes, we will get it done…in a bit. We need to finish some work first, Elfu-Pelfu.' He sounded like a harassed mother promising candy later to her clamouring children…knowing perfectly well that 'later' would never come.

Kumaragupta kept toddling ahead and turning back, waiting for the others to catch up.

Prabhavati called out to the energetic toddler. 'Kumu! Come back, baby! Stay close to me.' He gave her a mischievous look and ran full speed ahead, right onto the main road.

Suddenly there was a loud trumpet. As the others looked on, they saw a massive elephant – pinkish white in colour – waving its trunk wildly and charging down the road at full tilt. In its mindless panic, it was flattening everything in its path like a tornado…something had clearly spooked it.

And little Kumaragupta was directly in its path.

• • • • • • • • • • • • • • •

After a horrified split second, Rohan began to run as fast as he could towards the little boy. Prabhavati was just behind him, her face a picture of terror.

There was no way they would reach him in time.

Out of nowhere, someone leapt onto the street, whisking the confused toddler out of the elephant's path and putting him down gently in front of the group.

'Thank you sooo much,' exclaimed Prabhavati shakily.

'It is my pleasure,' a young man said suavely, in accented Sanskrit. He was dressed differently from the people around him with all their free-flowing cloth. He wore a full-sleeve long tunic with a broad cloth waistband and fitting trousers underneath.

'Oh, it looks sort of like a kurta-pyjama,' exclaimed Noor in one of her loud whispers.

Zoya looked at him consideringly. 'Hmm, is he a Rajput of some kind? Check out the facial hair,' she said, pointing at his luxuriant moustache and neatly trimmed beard.

Ansh giggled. 'Oh. My. God!!! What is THAT on his head?!' They looked up and saw that he had on a floppy, pointy triangular cloth hat – looking for all the world like some sort of ancient wannabe Santa Claus!

After its full-powered charge, the out-of-control elephant had slowed right down. It stood still, looking around. Its eye fell on Elfu and it wandered over, sniffing around the teenage elephant with its trunk.

Rohan exclaimed, 'Hey, this elephant has a faint pink star on its forehead – just like Elfu!'

Noor said, 'But look at its blush-pink skin…it's so light!'

'It is a white elephant…just like Lord Indra's Airavata,' said Prabhavati admiringly. 'They are extremely rare and holy.' She turned to the stranger. 'You don't seem to be from around here…are you part of the Shaka troupe?' she asked eagerly. 'I was just heading to see them.'

'Oh, it seems the young lady has heard of us,' he replied gracefully. 'Yes. I am. I am Virdaman. I was just going to get some flowers to decorate the horses before the show starts. We love them like our own children, you know. Sometimes better…at least they don't answer back!' He laughed at his own joke. Noor and Ansh rolled their eyes. Adults invariably thought they were so funny. Some things didn't change across the centuries!

Little Kumaragupta, meanwhile, had thoroughly enjoyed his new 'game', happily oblivious to all the drama and danger he'd been through. He turned to the light-coloured elephant and said, 'Again! Again! Play!'

Prabhavati glared at him and said, 'Come here, you little menace! You are staying right next to me.' She gave him a tight hug of relief and clutched on to his hand firmly.

He shook her off and wandered over to Elfu. Grabbing his trunk with his small hands, he said 'Up, *gaja*, up!' Elfu started wriggling his trunk to try and get this pint-sized nuisance off him.

'Humans...who'd have them!' groaned the white elephant delicately. 'I'm Madhumati,' it harrumphed in soft tones.

Oh my! Elfu was struck by the vision in front of him. He'd never seen another elephant like this. She was beauuuutiful – her skin had a pale pink blush...and was painted all over with a charming golden-and-blue lotus design. And right in the middle of her forehead was a little pink star...just like his! She even had long golden earrings that swung delicately as she ambled along.

He responded, 'Madhumati...the Honeyed One! That's such an apt name! You *do* look very sweet.' She gave him a sideways look.

'In fact, may I call you Honey?' Elfu added bashfully.

Her trunk fiddled with one of her long earrings coyly. 'That should be Honey-ji to you, I think – we barely know each other...!'

'So, Madhu, I mean Honey-ji, where are you from? And where did you get all your decorations? The paintings on you are eggggs-guisite...' Elfu harrumphed softly.

Madhumati was always pleased to find a new admirer. She fluttered her eyelashes.

'I am from a distant land. I came here on a floating house, you know. Across many oceans...it is very green and lush where I was. I lived in a palace...like my mother and grandmother and great-grandmother...'

'Wow, you are a Princess-elephant!' Elfu looked at her with shining eyes.

All that the children and Prabhavati could see was that Elfu and the white elephant were curiously sniffing each other with their trunks, and harrumphing periodically.

Ansh sniggered. 'Looks like that elephant's smitten.'

Noor turned to him fiercely. 'Let him be! And stop calling him "that elephant, that elephant!" He's our Elfu!'

• • • • • • • • • • • • • • •

Turning away from the elephants, Virdaman said to Prabhavati, 'I am heading back to the horse show. You are welcome to join me.'

She smiled delightedly. 'Yes! That would be great.' She turned to the children and said, 'Why don't you come along too? It will be a show you won't ever forget, that's what I've heard!'

Zoya hissed from the side of her mouth in English, 'Let's not lose her, guys!'

And so, the odd little group – five teens and two elephants – led by the Shaka warrior – made their way out of the market.

Noor bounded up to Prabhavati and started chatting with her. She rather liked this young royal, who seemed to be as energetic and fond of sports as she was. 'So, Princess, what is the physical training you do?'

Prabhavati replied, 'Hmm. My stepmother is so OBSESSED with me mastering the 64 *kala*s, it's really too much.' She rolled her eyes. 'Well, I don't mind learning mathematical puzzles or architecture or the art of writing ciphers or tongue-twisters, but I detest making flower necklaces…and learning to play music on tumblers filled with water is the WORST!

Noor looked at her wide-eyed. Architecture one day and musical glasses the next? The ancients were crazy!

'Do you ride horses too?' she ventured. 'You seem to love them…'

Prabhavati replied, 'Well, I learn horse riding, *obviously*. But also archery, sword fighting and general fitness.' She sighed. 'I do hope the Vakatakas will let me continue at least some of it.'

'The Waka-whos?' asked Noor, puzzled.

Prabhavati gave her a sideways look and raised her eyebrows incredulously. 'The Vakataka royal family?' At Noor's blank look, she said a little huffily, 'Oho. Seems you are really out of touch up there in Kashmir. I thought it was a big, famous university area! You know, Va.Ka. Ta.Kas? Rulers of the Deccan and the Maharashtrakas?'

The Waka Wakas? Shakira was here? Ansh began humming the famous song.

Prabhavati looked up at him and said with a smile. 'Yes, do sing one of your troupe's songs for me!'

Ansh abruptly stopped humming. He gave panicky looks to the other three. *Now what? What on earth was he supposed to sing? An ancient song from Kashmir? Aiiii...*

His brow cleared as an idea struck him, and he took a deep breath and launched right in.

'Tsamina Mina eh eh
Waka waka eh eh
Tsamina mina zangalewa
This time for Africaaaa!'

Noor and Ansh started doing the steps. Hands folded in a namaste, hips and neck swinging from side to side. Folded hands, and up and down. And again. Repeat the chorus, even louder!

Prabhavati stopped suddenly, jolted out of her self-absorption. 'What. Are. You. Doing! What IS that noise... that is not Sanskrit...'

Oh, here we go again. Zoya mentally rolled her eyes. She barely made the effort to glare at Ansh and Noor... they were always getting caught out each time they went back to the past!

She smiled hesitantly. 'Actually, you know in the north, you know where we are from...the far, very distant north? This is how we do our morning singing practice.'

'Hmm, really? Everyone does that?' asked the princess dubiously.

'Yes, yes.' They all nodded eagerly.

'Well, then, what is Ah-fricaah?' She stretched out the word.

Rohan jumped in. 'Why, that's the name of our village!'

'Yes, yes, we are from the village of Africaah in Kashmir,' added Noor.

Ansh felt the giggles come on. Until he felt a hard poke into his side as Zoya hissed, 'Don't even think about it, Ansh Desai! You're the one who got us into this trouble in the first place.'

•••••••••••••••

Rohan noticed his surroundings with interest. They were walking on a broad, cobbled road with gutters running alongside. On either side of the street stood tall residences painted with white limestone, dotted with big windows fitted with wooden shutters. These large houses were surrounded by gardens with gorgeous flowering trees.

Pigeons fluttered overhead, settling on the top floors where grain had been scattered for them.

The group was sharing the busy road with not just other pedestrians, but elephants carrying noblemen, chariots drawn by two or four horses, palanquins, and horse-riding soldiers patrolling the city.

They turned and left the wealthy neighbourhood, walking for a while before reaching a gateway.

Virdaman turned and said, 'The sports arenas are outside the main city, so we will go out this boundary gate.'

Zoya gazed at the enormous three-storey gateway made of wood and bamboo as they passed through. Soldiers, some on the parapet above, stood guarding it. They stepped onto a creaky wooden drawbridge, crossing a large moat filled with lotuses. A few ducks glided along placidly.

She turned to look back. The city was enclosed within a high, thick wooden wall that stretched out on both sides as far as she could see, with soldiers walking up and down on patrol, swords hanging from their belts and long spears in their hands.

'Ah – here we are…welcome – hope you enjoy it,' said Virdaman graciously, as they turned into a busy arena.

• • • • • • • • • • • • • • •

'OH. MY. GOD. That was crazyyyy.' Noor turned to Prabhavati with shining eyes.

'What a show! And those uniforms!' The princess agreed with an awestruck smile.

There had been a troupe of 40 Shakas – 20 men and 20 women. They were all dressed in trousers and boots with embroidery and bead work, with tunics made of exotic scale-armour – glinting golden metal scales over a red leather base – almost blindingly shiny under the bright sun. They wore tall, curved headgear studded with golden animal-shaped brooches.

And the horses! Even their decorations took ostentation to another level – each horse also wore a headdress! Each was tall and elaborate in a variety of designs – some shaped like curved antelope horns, others like stag antlers. They also wore loops of chains, and jewellery, and bolstered saddles.

There was music and drumming as the horses lined up with their riders on them, sitting ramrod straight. And then they started riding.

Time seemed to stop. Horse and rider became one. As they went racing across the field, the riders stood up in their saddles and began to shoot arrows from smallish wooden bows, pulling them out from strangely shaped quivers hanging from their waists on the left.

Two riders came to the fore and began shooting incredibly fast.

Ansh exclaimed, 'They are moving so fast that their fingers are blurry!'

Virdaman replied, 'Yes, we are the fastest in the world. We can shoot an arrow every five seconds!'

Another man went to the very end of the field and exited it, riding away furiously until he became a tiny speck in the distance. Another came up and asked the audience to quieten. As the large audience watched in pin-drop silence, there was a collective gasp as an arrow flew by, embedding itself in a target at the end of the field!

Rohan gasped. 'That must be half a kilometre…how could he even see it, much less aim at it?'

He turned to Virdaman in confusion. 'But these arrows seem to be awfully small and light…do they pierce that hefty armour?'

Virdaman smiled and replied. 'You are correct, young man. But they don't need to pierce very deep…for these are poison-tipped arrows! Made with a unique toxin of venom, human blood and faeces! Most victims are dead within an hour…and quite painfully. If the convulsions and vomiting don't get you, the rotting flesh and gangrene surely will.' He smiled gruesomely.

Urgh. Ansh shuddered. He couldn't figure out if he was more repulsed or scared.

He turned away from the Shaka and back to the show.

It was time for the women riders. They came galloping, standing up in their saddles. After a few rounds, they began to slip over the side, the horses still going incredibly fast.

'Oh my god, I can't watch!' exclaimed Zoya. As she watched through her fingers, the women riders turned upside down and began shooting arrows with their feet!

'WHAT!' she shouted in excitement. 'They are hitting their targets too! Nuts!'

Virdaman looked very pleased at this. 'Well, we are the Horse Lords.'

The children couldn't believe what they had seen. As they chattered excitedly, a loud voice pierced the air, from a slight distance away.

'STOP! STOP RIGHT THERE! I SEE YOU!'

The children gulped.

Were they caught?

• • • • • • • • • • • • • • • •

'Princess! Stop, Princess! There you are...' A tall, fair, muscular European woman hurried up. 'And with the little prince! I knew you'll be here, you horse-mad girl. Come along before I tell your father on you.' She held on to Prabhavati's arm with a vice-like grip, as if scared that she would disappear in a puff of smoke.

'Ouch! Gerrtorfmeeee, Helena, I'm coming.' Sulkily, Prabhavati tried to wriggle away.

'Anything could have happened,' the female bodyguard said agitatedly. 'And look at you, walking around in the sun without even an umbrella. What will happen to your complexion? Your mother will have me chopped up into a million little pieces!'

'Helena always gets so worked up over nothing,' explained Prabhavati, looking a bit sheepish.

'Come now, the face painter, the hairdresser, the flower-braider, the dhoti draper...they are ALL waiting for you, Kumari. It's a big day for you today!'

Prabhavati replied sulkily, 'I don't want to get my face drawn on! I don't want to get all trussed up like a useless doll!' *Err, oops!* Noor and Zoya gave each other a look, their hands creeping up to their faces…they had quite enjoyed getting their faces painted.

As the guard clutched her arm firmly and marched her and her brother away, the princess turned her head and yelled out, 'Hope you can come today!'

Zoya started laughing. 'Wow, she's feisty! But what a stroke of luck – we know the king will be at this spring-festival-party-thingummy later today…perfect chance to grab that strand of hair.'

Rohan said, 'But first we'd better figure out who this elephant belongs to – if it really is a white elephant, it will be really rare and valuable…somebody will be looking for it!'

Virdaman was watching the scene curiously. He asked Rohan in tones of astonishment. 'Do my ears deceive me? Was this young lady the illustrious Princess Prabhavati Gupta of Magadha?'

Zoya laughed. 'Oh, yes. She had slipped away specifically to see this amazing horse show!'

The man hit his head in frustration. 'So stupid! So stupid! Missed my chance! And that little one was the crown prince?'

Noor asked curiously, 'Chance for what?'

He ignored her and muttered, 'Now I'll have to wait for the party this afternoon…'

Noor asked him, 'Wait, how do you know about the party?' A look of suspicion crossed her face.

The man noticed this, and his manner changed immediately. He started smiling widely and said, 'I am just a little disappointed I wasn't able to pay my respects properly to the prince and princess.'

The Shaka quickly reached into his pouch and took out some large laddoos. He offered one to Madhumati and one to Elfu with a smile. 'Here, this is what we feed the horses for a special tasty treat after their performance.' Elfu flung his laddoo into his mouth unceremoniously, while Madhumati took hers daintily, gracefully lifting her trunk with the sweet to her mouth. Elfu looked at the man with great affection and began to sniff him all over with his trunk. *Oo. Another laddoo. In a special pouch.* Elfu sneaked it out and plopped it in his mouth while Virdaman was speaking to Zoya.

'Well, we must go and find Madhumati's owner…'

The Shaka looked inclined to keep chatting, until one of his comrades came up and whispered something in his ear. He suddenly started feeling in the inside of his kurta in a panic. He began peering into it and then ran his hands over his chest again, evidently looking for something. He looked up and said with barely restrained alarm, 'Well, I will take your leave then, young people. Farewell!' He rushed off.

• • • • • • • • • • • • • • •

The four children and two elephants began trudging back toward the centre of town. They slowly made their way through crowds of people, jostling and rubbing against the heaving masses.

Elfu had eyes only for his new friend. He made sure he was walking as close as possible to her.

Now was the time to seal the deal. Stopping in his tracks, he harrumphed, 'Err, Honey-ji, I have something for you.' He held out his trunk with a flourish.

Something flashed brilliantly, catching Rohan's eye.

He stopped dead in his tracks and grabbed the elephant's trunk. 'Elfu! What do you have here?' He wrested the object from the trunk of a reluctant Elfu, whose dreams of a romantic afternoon in the bazaar – trunk-in-trunk with Madhumati – were rapidly getting truncated.

The other children gazed down at Rohan's hand with their mouths open – in it lay the most gigantic diamond ring they had ever seen! As Rohan held it out, they saw that its dome shape covered his palm almost entirely as it lay there, gleaming in the bright sunlight.

• • • • • • • • • • • • • • •

'ELFU!' exclaimed Rohan loudly, turning to the elephant. 'Where EVER did you get this from?!'

Elfu looked sheepish. He'd just been sniffing around. Was it *his* fault that his trunk had encountered this thing in the extra laddoo he'd cheekily sneaked out of that pouch on the moustachioed man's chest? This stone had almost taken a tooth off him! He'd just hidden it in his mouth to impress Madhumati – it was so sparkly and beautiful... *just like her*. He came back to the moment with a small harrumph and saw Rohan looking at him sternly.

The children started chattering all at once. 'Where did he get this from?' asked Noor incredulously.

'What is it, a gazillion carats?' added Ansh.

Noor shouted, 'How is this a *ring*? If I put it on, my finger itself would fall off!'

'Oh gosh, it must be from that Shaka guy! That's why he was feeling around his vest in such alarm and rushed away so suddenly.'

'But why was he hiding this priceless ring inside his clothes?'

'This *has* to belong to royalty – there is no way a jewel this size belongs to an ordinary person.'

A cacophony of exclamations from the children started building up. Elfu took advantage of this distraction to twine his trunk around Madhumati's.

Suddenly, there was a loud 'SILENCE!' in a loud, quivering voice in accented Sanskrit from behind them. It continued: 'Unhand this holy elephant at once!'

The children stopped talking in sheer surprise. They turned and saw an elderly man, who had clearly been powerful in his youth, dressed in a simple dhoti of very fine white silk. He had relatively simple gold jewellery on – earrings, a gold chain and bracelets. His high cheekbones made him look sort of South-East Asian, though his skin tone was a deep brown. He was glaring at them through narrow eyes under his grey eyebrows.

A small entourage of men came rushing up to him, holding out unsheathed swords and sharp-tipped spears.

'Sorry, what?' said Rohan.

The old man continued in a threatening tone. 'I am Gangaraja, the King of Champa. Was the King of Champa. Whatever. This is my priceless white elephant Madhumati, my inseparable companion since she was born. You are thieves and kidnappers, and you shall be punished! I shall have you put to death!' He trembled in indignation.

At these words, the armed men advanced threateningly towards the children.

'No, no!' shouted Rohan 'You have it all wrong, sir! This crazy elephant, I mean, your precious Madhumati, she was charging down the marketplace! She almost crushed a child. She made friends with our elephant, and we were just coming to find out whom she belongs to!'

The old man continued to look outraged for a moment, before sighing and relaxing his stance. He made a gesture for his men to stand down. 'That actually doesn't surprise me...she's always been so high-spirited and vivacious.' He went up to the white elephant. 'Oh, Madhumati, you gave me a fright! You need to stop behaving like a child now – what would your mama Paramsundari say if she saw you behave this way!' The elderly king caressed the white elephant's trunk fondly. She simpered and wound her trunk around his neck lightly.

Ansh sniggered and said softly in English, '"High-spirited"?! She's spoilt rotten and cray-cray! More like Madhu-MAD-i!' He rotated his forefinger near his forehead.

Noor whispered back with a smirk, 'I'm sure that's what your mom says about youuuu, Ansh!' He made a face back at her but fondly. There was nothing they enjoyed more than annoying each other!

The king turned to the children. 'I do apologize for the confusion. I can't thank you enough. I don't know what I would do without Madhu...her family has been with us for centuries! An unbroken line of white elephants...I was planning to ride her this afternoon to the Vasantotsav and engagement party for Samrat Chandragupta Vikramaditya's daughter ...'

Zoya's ears pricked up. *He was going to meet Emperor Chandragupta this afternoon?*

'Come, you must let me thank you by inviting you for a meal...well, some snacks, anyway...'

As they protested, he added, 'I want to meet and learn *all* about the common people of this country...and you children look *so very* common.' He smiled beatifically.

Err...what? 'That kind of sounded like a compliment, but I don't think it was!' whispered Noor to Zoya in English, trying not to break into giggles.

Ansh chimed in, 'It was an insultement! A compliment which is really an insult. LOL.'

They immediately started squabbling. 'No one actually says the letters LOL when they speak, Ansh.' Noor rolled her eyes.

'Oh yeah, who made you the Leader of Gen Z?' he shot back.

Meanwhile, the king grabbed Rohan's arm and started doddering purposefully down a road, muttering, 'We must drop off darling Madhu first...'

•••••••••••••••

Soon they entered a section of the city that felt really alien.

'Wow, WHERE are we?' wondered Noor. 'It doesn't feel like India…are we in Singapore or Dubai?' She gazed around wonderingly. There were foreigners everywhere. Shaven-headed monks in various autumnal coloured robes of yellow, orange or red were walking around with their bowls. Ahh! Buddhist monks. So. Many. Buddhist monks. Maybe one out of three people looked Indian.

King Gangaraja said, 'Yes, this is the Foreigners' Quarter of Magadha. Not only people from our side of the world, but also – see those – Persians! Greeks! Romans!' He pointed to a group of fair, dark-haired men with beards, wearing…were those long dresses and short dresses?

'My courtiers were insisting I stay with a nobleman of high rank, but I want to *absorb* the essence of India, I want to *breathe* in its pure and holy air. It has been my dream to come here for *so many* years…and now I'm finally here…' King Gangaraja sighed and took a deep breath just as a passing horse decided to expel a particularly aromatic pile of dung.

As he started gagging and coughing, Zoya and Noor tried to stifle their snorts of laughter.

By now they had reached an impressive-looking two-storeyed mansion. It had a large group of South-East Asian men wearing short dhotis and turbans standing around chatting with one another.

'Ahem. Ahem.' The king cleared his throat loudly.

Startled, they looked up. As soon as they saw the elderly king, all the guards rushed over and, crossing their hands over their chests, bowed deeply from the waist. Two men who had been slouching near the gate straightened up and started blowing conches in the air. A drummer began to beat out a rhythm hastily.

'No, no. Stop. STOP.' King Gangaraja said crankily in Sanskrit. 'How many times have I said, none of this here any more! I have renounced my kingdom.'

An attendant rushed over with a large cotton parasol, exclaiming '*Om namah-shivaya*! O mighty king, you left so suddenly…here, let me offer you some shade.'

'*Om namah-shivaya*. No, no, Kandarpadharma. Let me be. I am learning to be a common person. These children are teaching me how.'

The children were watching with some bemusement. This king was too much!

'At least wear your crown, O King!' Another attendant rushed over and tried to put a cylindrical gold crown atop the royal's head.

'Uffo! Get away! I have just come to drop off Madhumati. I found her at last. Please take her. I am going to visit an inn to dine like a peasant now!' King Gangaraja sounded very excited by the thought.

Elfu, however, was watching with dismay. Surely this couldn't be the end of the road for him and Honey? He harrumphed softly in distress, reaching out his trunk towards Madhumati. She gave him a misty-eyed look and reached her trunk out as well, the two entwining.

'Well, this is sad. But it was nice meeting you, Mr…whatsyername?'

'Elfu,' he said shyly.

'I must go...Mr Elfu. What an...interesting name... but...go I must...'

The attendants led Madhumati away gently, scolding her teasingly. 'Come on, Madhu! Another conquest?' As she turned her head for a last look at Elfu, the other one laughed – 'Incorrigible!'

Elfu watched as she was led to the other side of the gate and was gradually lost from view. *Wait! He could still hear her on the other side of the wall.* He cocked his large flappy ear. He heard a chorus of harrumphs as Madhumati rejoined her elephant companions.

'Oh, Madhu! Where did you goooo...we missed you.'

'The king went into a fit when he found out you'd slipped away! How are you still his favourite with all the stunts you pull!'

She tinkled a little harrumph. 'Well, you know me, I need to explore.'

'So, tell us...what did you do? Whom did you meet?' Elfu heard another elephant asking.

'Oh, nothing much. Saw some horse stunts. Otherwise, quite average.' Elfu strained his ears, waiting for her to mention him and their special bond.

'What have y'all been up to?' Elfu heard munching sounds as Madhu presumably began snacking on some hay.

He turned away dejectedly. She didn't care! Even a little bit!

•••••••••••••••

Leaving his fawning attendants behind with some difficulty, King Gangaraja led the four youngsters and a crestfallen Elfu a little further down the road.

'Come, come! I have been waiting to try this local *bhojanalaya*, but my attendants keep cooking feasts for me at home to dissuade me!'

'So, where are you from, O King?' Zoya asked him curiously. Though his manners and dress were Indian, he seemed exotic.

'Why, I am from the fabled Suvarnabhumi…the Golden Land…Praise be to Shiva.' He smiled with satisfaction. At their look of confusion, he sighed. 'It's shocking how few people have heard of us…why, we are constantly speaking of Bharatavarsha in Simhapura!'

'I am the king…ahem, sorry!…the former king of the mighty kingdom of Champa! It is a green, lush land far away. We had to sail for months to reach here…'

Zoya half-turned her back and surreptitiously clicked the History of India app on her phone, hastily typing in 'Kingdom of Champa.' Her eyes widened as she read the entry.

'Guys! That's Vietnam! This dude is from Vietnam.' Everyone's eyes grew big. How could this person with such an Indian name and such Indian manners be from VIETNAM?

King Gangaraja was saying, 'My esteemed father was Dharmamaharaja Sri Bhadravarman. Great man. Immense scholar. He knew all the four *Vedas* by heart. A true Shiva *bhakta*. He built so many *devalayas*...what do you say, temples...'

'So why did you give up your kingdom, Mr King?' asked Noor curiously.

'Well,' he said, 'though I am not as scholarly as my dear departed father, I always wanted to come and live out my days on the banks of the holiest of rivers, Mother Ganga...so I decided to do just that!' The children looked stupefied.

'In fact, in a few days I am heading to Kashi to be close to both the Ganga and my lord Shiva...I am impatient to feel the peace and comfort I am sure I will over there...'

'Whoooooaa!' exclaimed Ansh. 'You gave up your kingdom to come and spend your life in Kashi??!'

'Yes, well, the Chinese were annoying me, anyway! Kept demanding more and more elephants every year... And then when the revered Brahmins came to my capital Simhapura on the ship along with traders, my longing became too great to ignore. The Funanese king's expression should be a sight!'

He tutted at their bewildered faces. 'Indians don't know much about us! Funan! The large kingdom next to ours?

They may be richer in wealth, but I am surely richer in dharma and karma by this action!' He chuckled.

'Come, we have reached.' King Gangaraja stopped in front of a bustling building.

It was a huge hall, open to the River Ganga on one side, with the breeze wafting through. It was interspersed with wooden pillars, intricately carved with leafy creepers and birds. The walls were painted with lifelike scenes of Pataliputra.

'I'll get a place to keep your *gaja*.' He spoke to the owner, a harried-looking man, who was rushing about. The man gestured to an attendant, who came and started leading Elfu along the side to the back of the building. They all followed.

'Oh!' exclaimed Rohan. They were right on the banks of the River Ganga – wide and flowing rapidly – you couldn't see far into its grey depths. He attached a flimsy rope to Elfu's ankle and whispered, 'Stay here, mister. I'll be back soon…' When he saw the elephant's sad expression, he added, '…and maybe with some tasty treats!'

Treats?! Hmm, a nice fried samosa or two would go far in helping fill the sad, hollow feeling in his stomach, thought Elfu mournfully.

The group walked back to the front and rejoined King Gangaraja, who led them inside.

The children walked through the room, passing people sitting on low couches with thick mattresses and bolsters placed on them, flanked by small low tables. Bowls with fragrant flowers were scattered around the room. He chose an area that faced the river, where hanging tapestries separated sections from one another.

The king sat with them.

An attendant came up and asked, 'What'll you 'ave then? To drink we have *shikharini*...or the hard stuff...'

The king said hastily 'No, no, no alcohol! *Shikharini* for them, please.'

'And to eat?' the other man enquired. 'We only have *vataka* and *modak*...'

The king sighed. 'Plenty of each, then...and might it be possible to get some plain khichri for me?'

Zoya and Ansh looked at each other. Would khichri never leave them alone?! In any age they travelled to?

A wizened Buddhist monk in dark-red robes came up. He had a shaven head and a long white beard. He was holding a stout and tall walking stick. 'O King, what an honour seeing you here...never seen you in this restaurant before...' He too spoke Sanskrit, but with a curious accent.

'I am sampling indigenous delights,' replied King Gangaraja graciously.

'Yes, well, everything in Bharata is wondrous...it is the homeland of our most beloved Shakyamuni after all,' replied the monk.

'Shaka who? The Shakas we met?' Ansh asked Zoya in a whisper.

'Ansh!! What on earth you do in History cl...' she trailed off. 'Okay, fine, this isn't THAT obvious actually,' she admitted. 'In a nutshell, the Buddha was also called the Shakyamuni as he belonged to a tribe called the Shaa-

KYaas, which is different from the Shaa-Kaas we met. End of explanation.' She wiggled her eyebrows at him. He wiggled them back with a grin. 'Thanks, Zany Zo…I mean Encyclopaedia Zoannica.'

The monk was saying, 'It is always a pleasure to meet the ruler of the kingdom of Champa…we would love to introduce the righteous path there…'

'Please meet…actually, young ones, I don't know your names yet – well, this is the revered Buddhist monk all the way from China, known as Shih Faxian. He has come on a pilgrimage to this great country, much like I have, though a different one.' He smiled at the monk.

The old monk smiled and asked the children, 'And your names are?

Rohan got an unexpectedly mischievous grin and pattered off, 'I am Rohanaditya…this is Anshaditya…' and looking at the girls for a split second, continued, 'This is Noormati…and Jayamati!' Ansh whispered in English to the girls, 'And you both are varieties of the famous Basmati!' – looking delighted at his own joke.

'Hmm, these are unusual names – where are you from?' asked Faxian curiously.

The children used their earlier story. 'Why, we are from the far north. Kashmir, you know.'

'Ah, Kashmir! Indeed, I DO know. I was there just a few years ago! Great centre for Buddhism. Famous for it. Which part exactly?'

Uh-oh. Caught. Now what?!

•••••••••••••••

'Oh, we will, but, Mr Faxian, please, please first tell us of what you have seen,' pleaded Zoya. She needed to get his attention off them, pronto!

Seeing Zoya's desperation, Noor also jumped in. 'And how on earth did you come from China, Mr Faxian? That's sooo far away...'

The monk turned to them with a smile. He did love to chat with Indians...the fellow compatriots of his beloved and revered Shakyamuni.

'Well, how did I come? Young lady, I walked. And I walked. And I walked.'

Noor's eyes widened. 'You walked from China?'

'Why, yes, we have been walking for the past five years.'

'The Buddha said to his monks, "*Charaiveti, charaiveti...*" – keep walking...and so I do.'

'I was happy to see so many Buddhist monasteries and stupas all along the way – Udayana, Gandhara, Takshashila...even the lofty stupa of King Kanishka at Purushpura.' He smiled in delight. 'It was grand...four hundred cubits high. You know a cubit? About this much.' He gestured from his elbow to the tip of his middle finger.

Rohan told the others, 'Ohhh, about 500 feet then...that's huge!' From the corner of his eye, he saw King Gangaraja slip away to chat with some other people in the room.

'Yes,' said the old monk admiringly, 'It is commonly called the finest stupa in Jambudvipa.

'My heart is at peace in the land of the Shakyamuni. I have seen where he shaved his head and clipped his nails...where he is said to have gouged out one of his eyes to give to a blind...'

Ansh interrupted before things got even more graphic. 'And what have you noticed about the people you met, Mr Faxian?'

Faxian came out of his reverie. 'Amazing. This country is incredible. Neither frost nor snow. Everyone is happy and following the dharma. No decapitation and no beatings... truly incredible!

'Imagine. Throughout the whole country the people do not kill any living creature, nor drink intoxicating liquor, nor eat onions or garlic. No butchers' shops and no wine shops. We must do the same back home.'

Rohan said in an aside to Zoya with a grin. 'Well, safe to say he seems to be the Number One fan of India!'

Faxian looked set to extol the virtues of India in much more detail, but his attention was called to another Buddhist monk and he hustled off.

• • • • • • • • • • • • • • •

The food arrived. King Gangaraja came by and said hurriedly, 'My young friends, eat all you want. I must rush off on an urgent errand. But enjoy the food to your heart's content. And thanks again for saving my beloved Madhu!' He rushed off without waiting for an answer.

'Oh gosh!' groaned Zoya. 'Now what?! We were going to try and go along to the party as part of his entourage.'

Ansh said, busily tucking into a sweet *modak*, 'Let's eat first. The food's great. And free! Beats wheatgrass and banana smoothies – my daily breakfast…'

Zoya slurped some of the thick drink made of yoghurt, cardamom, sugar and camphor. 'This…what is it called… *shikharini* is just delicious…so refreshing.'

Noor pounced on the *vataka*s, which turned out to be *vada*s.

'Hahaha,' chuckled Rohan. 'I should take some *vada*s for Elfu too. Poor thing, he's looking rather woebegone since his separation from Mad Madhu!'

As they chowed down the snacks at a steady rate, they saw two South-East Asian looking monks behind them starting to argue.

'EVERYone knows Thailand is Suvarnabhumi...the Golden Land!'

The other burst in 'No-oh! No way. It's Funan and there's no debate, even.'

The argument got louder and louder, until a third monk came up and said, 'Calm down, brothers. Calm down. I will tell you the answer.'

They turned to him expectantly. He smirked and said, 'Come on. Everyone knows it's Burma – that's Suvarnabhumi!'

The children grinned and rolled their eyes. Guess you didn't grow out of some things when you grew up.

Rohan suddenly put his finger on his lips and pointed to the half screen that was separating them from another table. The children tried to concentrate and pay attention over the general hubbub. They could glimpse flashes of the people sitting there but not see them properly.

'Virdaman, where could the ring have gone?' asked a male voice worriedly, in an unusual-sounding language. 'We were supposed to use it to break up this Vakataka–Gupta alliance, that was our mission.'

A familiar voice replied, 'I really don't know. I had it tucked away so safely inside that laddoo against my chest.'

The kids' mouths dropped open. *What?! And OMG, they still had the ring!* They had completely forgotten about it.

The first man carried on, 'So now what?'

Virdaman replied loudly, 'What else? We will have to activate plan B...cut the tree from its root...no king, no alliance!'

His companion shushed him, saying, 'Softer, softer, someone will hear you!'

Virdaman laughed shortly. 'That's our secret weapon, Ushavadata…no one can understand a word we are saying in the Shaka language here!'

The children looked at each other, wild-eyed. Noor pointed incredulously at the screen, mouthing, 'The Shakas!' Zoya warned her with her finger on her lips to remain silent. It was imperative that the Shakas didn't know they were sitting right next to them.

Suddenly a bunch of guards burst in. One shouted, 'Everyone stay where you are! Don't move! We will search you. The priceless Syamantaka ring has gone missing from the palace. Don't any of you try any stunts!'

The man next to Virdaman said in his own language, 'Look, what should we do now?'

Virdaman replied, 'Well, we don't have the ring, do we? Be calm and keep your nerve!'

The kids were terrified. If they were caught, a horrid, nasty death awaited for sure. The ring was in Rohan's pouch!

They were sitting towards the back of the building, close to a terrace overlooking the river from a height. Rohan silently sidled off towards the balcony. As the guards made their way around the tense room, sending plates of food flying with violent disregard, one by one the other children joined Rohan outside.

It was at least 10 feet higher than the water, and above where Elfu was standing…

'What should we dooo?'

'Should we just confess?' asked Ansh nervously.

'Ha! Not likely! These soldiers look the sort to kill first, ask questions later,' scoffed Noor.

Rohan started calling out to Elfu from the side of the balcony. 'Come Elfu-Pelfu, come to Rohan.'

Elfu looked piteously at the skimpy rope tying his leg to an iron ring.

Rohan urged, 'Break it, Elfu, it's very weak.' As he kept gesturing and urging, Elfu finally tried lifting his leg and the rope snapped off effortlessly. Elfu looked up and gave Rohan a wounded look for tricking him, and lumbered over slowly.

Rohan said urgently 'Noor, come here! Try to get on Elfu's back and slide down his trunk.' The most athletic of the lot, she came over. She shimmied down the balcony a bit and managed to get on to Elfu's back. He jumped a little but managed to not move a lot. As Zoya came over to do the same, suddenly a man burst onto the balcony, brandishing a sword.

'Stop! In the name of the emperor, stop!'

Rohan looked up with a gulp. As he backed up, the man advanced.

'No,' he said with desperate courage.

The soldier rushed and Rohan, who retreated furiously, realized he had stepped into…nothing.

He went hurtling through the air backwards.

•••••••••••••••

Rohan hit something with a hard smack. Suddenly he realized it was water. He'd made it to the Ganga! With his limbs intact!

He shouted, 'Elfu, come here! Bring Zoya and Noor.'

Elfu had looked alarmed when he saw Rohan in the river, being carried off by the current. He started trotting at a brisk pace, leaving Noor and Zoya to try and hold on for dear life. He soon entered the Ganga and began swimming. The girls were swept off his back, and were carried along swiftly by the churning water.

Noor and Zoya shouted, 'JUMP! Ansh! Jump! Go on!'

Ansh had been standing, feeling stunned by this turn of events. At Noor and Zoya's urging, he looked below. It seemed like a l-o-o-o-ong way down. The water was moving fast. What should he do? He hesitated.

The soldier started approaching Ansh threateningly. 'Go on!' he said. 'There is no way you are going to jump, you snivelly little snot!'

Ansh closed his eyes and jumped with blind trust. He went deep into the swirling waters, and came back up, gasping.

Uff. Strong current! He couldn't think as he was carried along rapidly.

He was just trying to avoid breathing in water or hitting any rocks. As he tried to get his bearings, the river turned a bend, and the water slowed down and became placid.

Ansh looked around. He was right in the middle of the river. The banks on either side looked really far away. This was scary. Aah! He turned and saw Noor quite close to him. Phew!

The duo soon spotted Rohan and Zoya, who were swimming close to each other.

Elfu had caught up as well and was swimming along gamely. They somehow managed to manoeuvre so they were closer to one another, though still in the middle of this wide river.

Suddenly, Rohan felt a bump. 'Ouch. Was that you?'

Zoya replied, irritated, 'No, of course not! Ouch! What was that?!'

As they looked, they saw a small body jump up, a long thin snout showing briefly before it went back into the grey water.

'Wait. Was that...a...shark?? What the heck! There can't be sharks in the Ganga, for heaven's sake!'

'Don't be silly. Sharks don't have snouts like that...was that a baby dolphin?' asked Zoya wonderingly.

Rohan panted out, 'Guys! I think these are river dolphins...and I don't think they are particularly friendly!'

Soon they were getting bumped left, right and centre.

'Ouch! You bullies!' cried out Noor.

'Uh, I think they're blind,' said Rohan.

'Blind or not, I thought dolphins were friendly,' wailed Ansh, trying to swim and breathe, and avoid these very-not-nice creatures who kept butting him with their snouts!

Suddenly, he saw a rope coming through the air and landing next to him. He looked over and saw a large barge-type boat being rowed by eight oarsmen. There were a few men standing on its deck. One of them had thrown the rope. The man shouted, 'Hold tight!'

Ansh clutched it and felt himself being pulled swiftly towards the boat, squealing as he was dragged roughly through the water. He was relieved when he was hauled up.

Before long, the other children were on deck as well, breathing heavily in relief.

Zoya muttered to Rohan, 'Look at Elfu! Looks a little miffed at not being invited onto the boat, but let's be fair. If he was on the boat, none of us would be. In fact, the boat itself wouldn't BE at all!' Rohan smiled but looked sympathetically at Elfu, who was swimming alongside the boat huffily. He did hate missing out!

'Welcome aboard, young ones!'

The children turned and saw a prosperous-looking young man, dressed in a simple silk dhoti and *uttariya*. He lacked most of the jewellery, paint and flowers they had come to expect in Gupta times.

'Hello,' they chorused. Noor added, 'Thank you for saving us. Those dolphins weren't being very nice.'

'You are welcome.' He grinned. 'Good thing it was *susus* and not the crocodiles, eh?' At Rohan's panicked look at Elfu, he laughed and said, 'I'm joking, of course!'

Ansh whispered, 'Dolphins were called *susu* in ancient India??? I can't even...' Zoya gave him a warning look while trying not to giggle.

The man said, 'I am Acharya Aryabhata, and who are you?'

Ping! Even Ansh had heard of the famous mathematician Aryabhata. And now they were sitting in his boat? This was legitimately crazy!

Zoya got very excited. No one knew much about Aryabhata and his life in modern times. This was her chance!

She started quizzing him at top speed. 'Where are you from and why are you on a boat in Pataliputra?'

He tried to keep up. 'I spent much of my youth in Kusumpura...just nearby, you know, but now I am the head of the university at...'

'Ujjain,' finished Zoya, nodding excitedly.

Aryabhata's pleasant and abstracted face turned red and scowling. 'How on earth did you know that I live in Ujjain now?'

As Zoya floundered, he added sharply, 'Oh no! Don't tell me this was all an elaborate ruse to get me to accept you as my pupil...I very specifically told everyone I'm not taking any more students for the next couple of years.' He groaned loudly, clutching his head in his hands.

'No, no, sire...believe me,' interjected Zoya.

'We are musicians from Kashmir...' said Ansh.

Zoya added, 'I had heard of you, of course, that is why. Your fame has spread far and wide.'

'MY "fame"?' Aryabhata asked suspiciously. 'Why would you lot care about some obscure mathematics? I'm hardly Kalidasa, or some famous musician.'

Hmm. Now what?

Noor jumped in. 'Sire, Jayamati *did* have an interest in academics back in Kashmir...in fact, she wanted to become ordained as a Buddhist *bhikkhuni* so she could keep studying in the sangha all her life – but circumstances were such... I often tell her that a shaved head would become her greatly...' she trailed off with an internal chuckle as she saw Zoya glaring at her.

'Hahaha! Sibling quarrels – I miss them,' said Aryabhata with a genuine laugh.

'So, how come you are here in Pataliputra, sir?' asked Rohan, to distract him further.

Aryabhata replied wryly, 'Well, I was here visiting family, and the emperor insisted I stay back for this Vasantotsav and engagement party. I told him it's not really my scene, but how do you say no to the emperor, right?!'

Noor smiled and said, 'In fact, we are also headed there, Acharya. As...err...' looking down at her bedraggled clothes, 'err...as helpers for the party.'

Aryabhata smiled kindly and said, 'That's good. Don't worry, I'm sure they will give you a set of acceptable clothes.'

Noor started laughing. They were in such a bad state that he was worried they wouldn't even be allowed to be 'servers'!

Aryabhata continued, 'So, anyway, here I am, but I just needed a few minutes to get away from everyone and work something out, so I borrowed a friend's boat and am slowly making my way towards that *shreshthi*'s house via river as I ponder...'

'What are you pondering, Acharya?' Ansh asked him curiously.

'Welllll...I'm composing a book, so various theories around that...' he looked dubious, reluctant to dive in.

Coaxed by the children, he happily started explaining his various theories.

'Well, I am pretty sure that Earth is spherical in shape... and it rotates. Round and round. That's why we have day and night. And I've calculated its circumference. One of my fellow mathematicians insists I'm crazy. But I'm right...I know it I'm right!' He looked at them defiantly as if expecting them to denounce his madness.

Ansh whispered to Zoya under his breath in English, 'Err...the Earth's rotation was a controversial opinion in ancient times? Okay...'

'And if you take any circle, right? Its circumference,' he drew it in the air with a finger, 'divided by its diameter,' he gestured again, '...it's always, always the same. And it's a long, long number. I've got 3.141 so far...by the grace of Brahma, I will get more...'

'OMG! Is he talking about pi?' whispered Ansh. He just couldn't resist. He had a T-shirt with the first 60 digits of pi! He started saying, 'Oh, it's 3.141...'

Whoop! Rohan pushed Ansh so he went flying and fell flat on the deck of the boat.

Rohan gestured with his hands and whispered in English, 'Bro! What you doing? We're supposed to be from the past, remember? You're not from the 21st century here!'

Ansh looked rather abashed. So excited he'd remembered something studies-related, he'd completely forgotten that he had access to way more information that any genius of the past!

Aryabhata continued on, 'And I firmly believe time is without beginning and without end. None of this creation of Earth and all that.'

'Wow!' muttered Noor. 'That's pretty modern.'

'And this is how to construct sine tables...'

As the great scholar eventually reached his theory of the epicyclic models of planetary motion, everyone's eyes had properly glazed over.

He looked over in dismay and stopped speaking, rousing them from their dreamlike trance. Zoya had never experienced such an information overload before...quite a novel sensation for her!

The great mathematician was saying glumly, 'Yes, people often get that particular look when I start!'

They rushed to comfort him. 'Acharya, we love listening to you. Please continue.'

'Haha! So polite. But, young ones, we have reached the docking point for the *shreshthi*'s house. It was so interesting to talk to you. Must say I enjoyed myself!'

'Aren't you coming with us?' asked Zoya, crestfallen.

'No...just a little while. The answer is close. I need to think...3.141...6? Or is there more?'

Aryabhata waved to them as they waded to the shore, Elfu struggling to get out and shake off the water. He did enjoy swimming. A mud bath would have been simply perfect.

As the boat drew away steadily, the children could see the great scholar become preoccupied in thought once again.

Rohan turned to Noor. 'Bet you that Aryabhata skips the party.' Noor replied with an indignant chuckle, 'Not a chance, I agree with you.'

Zoya said, a little dreamily, 'What a day it's been so far already! We've met Prabhavati Gupta, her brother, horse-riding Shaka stuntmen – and women – a Hindu Vietnamese king, a Chinese Buddhist monk…the great Aryabhata…what a day!'

Ansh muttered with a touch of snark, 'You didn't mention almost getting killed multiple times, Zozo.'

'Oho! C'mon, let's at least dry off before we try to find the *shreshthi*'s house…we look bedraggled, but if we're soaking wet, they won't even let us past the gates…' Zoya went and sat on a fallen tree trunk, closing her eyes and processing the day so far. The others all took spots near the bank, and Elfu began lazily grazing on some leaves.

They were bone dry within an hour, though looking considerably worse for the wear than when they had arrived in Pataliputra that morning.

As they walked up the side road from the river to one of the main roads of the neighbourhood, they saw people heading towards a particular house. Some held baskets of flowers, and others carried plates of fruits.

'Bingo! We got it,' said Noor happily, hurrying up to follow them. And soon there they were, standing in front of one of the largest mansions they had ever seen.

••••••••••••••••

As the children walked close, they heard a cacophony of trumpeting.

Just before the gates was a large corral-type structure with many stands that had iron chains in a row. These already had a few elephants attached to them, with their mahouts standing by.

'Aah!' said Rohan with satisfaction. 'We can park Elfu here...can hardly sneak him in with us!'

As he led Elfu in, Ansh burst out, 'Hahaha! Guys, actually, this is exactly like an elephant parking lot!'

Rohan stopped in his tracks and started laughing loudly. 'This is too funny! I need to tell my brother about this!'

'What on earth are you on about, Ro?' demanded Zoya.

'Well, when my brother Sunil went to the US, people used to ask him whether he went everywhere on elephants... and...whether...' – he stopped again, wheezing with laughter – 'whether...the elephants in India *had parking lots like they did for cars there*! And now I can say that I've seen an actual elephant parking lot!' He stood up straight. 'Well, at least I could theoretically say it if I could ever admit anything about our adventures out loud.'

• • • • • • • • • • • • • •

They walked up towards the house.

The guards gave them a pointed look and gestured to a side path. 'Go along there. And hurry! They have been waiting for you.'

'Wait, why are we being directed to the side?' whispered Noor in confusion. 'And what does he mean – they have been waiting for us?'

She stopped, as they had already entered an enormous garden stretching as far as their eyes could see in all directions. Flower beds hugged the sides, and large colourful trees dotted the landscape – the blazing red blossoms of *ashoka*, the bright yellow of *kadamba*, delicately perfumed yellow *champa* and fragrant jasmine creepers.

As they walked in, they saw water fountains cooling the air, and a large water tank with marbled steps leading into it on all four edges. Attendants were rushing about.

Peacocks strutted around, and monkeys looked down from the trees. There were one-, two- and three-seater swings simply everywhere. In the centre of the garden were low couches and silk, cotton-stuffed mattresses here and there. Bowls of betel leaves were kept on low tables. There was an air of hectic activity.

'So many swings!' exclaimed Zoya.

Only a few guests seemed to be there yet. The children stopped and stared around them mutely.

'Why is everyone wearing so much jewellery?' groaned Noor. Everyone was wearing dhotis and long scarves. And they had SO MUCH ELSE going on! Jewellery! Flowers! Face paint! There was no concept of too much in Gupta times, clearly.

Ansh began to count: 'Heaps of gold jewellery. Check! Heaps of flower jewellery. Check! Heaps of face paint. Check! Insane hairdos. Check! Check! Check!'

On the side, a low wooden stage had been raised, and simple decorations were being hastily put up. There was a large curtain set up as a screen towards the back.

A wiry man with a worried look was dashing about the stage, shouting frantic instructions in Sanskrit.

His hair was long and open, and he was clean-shaven. He wore a fine dhoti in printed fabric and a long, matching scarf around his neck. Like everyone else, he wore plenty of jewellery – earrings, necklace, armbands, anklets, bracelets, belt...all gold...but on the lighter side.

He saw the children and shouted, 'There you are! Where have you been? Come here AT ONCE!' At this, the youngsters were really taken aback. *Did he...could he know them?*

'Err...' said Rohan.

A plainly dressed young man hurried up to them. 'Come. You are late. You lot were supposed to be here two *prahars* ago! Shri Kalidasa has worked himself up into a panic by now! The play is due to be staged in less than one *prahar*!'

KALIDASA? Ansh and Noor gave wide-eyed looks to each other. HIM even they had heard of...especially in their Sanskrit classes!

'Which play, sir?' asked Ansh timidly.

The man gave an exasperated snort. 'The theatre people didn't tell you anything, hunh! Why, it's the long awaited first show of *Abhijnanashakuntalam*...the Recognition of

Shakuntala, you know! Everyone's been talking about it for ages!

'Anyway, hurry up and come along! Help with the final set-up of the stage and then change into your costumes... What are your names?' He started walking away hurriedly.

'Err... Jayamati, Noormati, Anshaditya, Rohanaditya...' ventured Zoya, cringing inside.

What sort of names were these?! The man gave her a look but strode away.

'Wait...they think we're ACTORS?' hissed Noor. 'What the heck are we going to do now?!'

Zoya gave her a resigned shrug and went off to the corner where the actors were getting ready. The others followed. The make-up artist gave them a quick once-over, and added flowers to their clothes, and simple face paint to Zoya and Noor's face before sending them off.

They made their way to the side of the stage.

The long-haired man came up to them, waving his arms anxiously. He moaned, 'Where is the mini-horse? And the trained pygmy deer? And the elephant? Do you *yuvaks* know anything about it?'

Eh, what now? Zoya said in bemusement, 'No, we don't, sire.' This must be the famous Kalidasa, she thought.

'But I *must* have a deer dart across the stage for the entrance and then the horse with the actor alongside it to show a hunt! All the beauty of the scene will be lost otherwise! And everyone will hate my play!' Kalidasa began pulling his hair in despair.

'No no, sire, you are so brilliant, everyone will love it.' soothed Zoya.

Noor jumped in. 'In fact, you are the Shakespeare of Bharat!'

'No, no,' added Ansh helpfully, 'Shakespeare was the Kalidasa of Britain!'

Kalidasa stopped his pacing and looked up in sheer astonishment. 'Shik-sa-peer? Bri-tah-nah?! What are you all on about? Where are you from?!'

Rohan stared at him mutely. Zoya thought, *not again*! and rushed in. 'Sire, we live in Pataliputra, but we are musicians from very far away. Very far north. Kashmir, sire.'

'Okayyyy.' He looked at them consideringly…and a little suspiciously. 'And who is Britahnah and where is Shik-sa-peer?'

'Err, he's a man, sire,' said Ansh feebly. 'Just a…guy. Writes plays like you. BUT NOT LIKE YOU, of course. You are so illustrious.' Sweat beaded his brow. Could they just get out of this time and back home already?

'And where is this great man?' enquired the playwright. 'I would like to meet him and…'

'Sadly, he's a recluse, sir. He lives in the kingdom north of ours, called Britain.'

Kalidasa looked miffed. 'Okay, tell me a dialogue of his.'

Ansh thought and loudly proclaimed: 'A horse, a horse, my kingdom for a horse!'

Kalidasa looked outraged. 'That's it? Not very expressive, is he? Speaking of which, WHERE IS MY HORSE?!' He turned to his secretary and exclaimed dramatically, 'My kingdom for a horse!'

'Err…sire, it is actually not *your* kingdom, it is Emperor Chandragupta's…' said the harassed secretary timidly.

The children tried to control their chortles as they saw Kalidasa's mighty frown.

'Off with his head!' added Ansh helpfully. He was enjoying himself by now.

'What? Shiksapeer said that too?'

'Actually, it was the Queen of Hearts from *Alice in Wonderland*...err...'

Kalidasa shook his head, muttering, 'Things are very different up in the north it seems...never mind, never mind, focus!'

He looked up at them and asked, 'What are your names anyway?'

Zoya cringed even harder. 'Jayamati, Noormati, Anshaditya, Rohanaditya.' Eep.

Kalidasa gave them a look, before saying, 'Okay, please go and get the rest of the flowers from the storerooms on the other side of the house.'

He turned back to his burdened secretary, 'We *must* have an elephant. But it can't be huge! Someone FIND ME A SMALL ELEPHANT!'

'Err, maestro?' ventured Rohan. 'I do have a pet elephant on the smaller side and he's quite obedient...if you'd like?'

'Perfect! First bit of good news today. Secretary! Follow me!' And off they went.

•••••••••••••••

Soon Elfu was installed behind the stage, feeling very chuffed to be a part of things again. It had been fun in the elephant parking lot, but he was getting a lot of FOMO about the human party!

'Right, so this elephant will be the king's fan bearer in the later scene…someone give him a fan to hold in his trunk,' instructed Kalidasa.

'Bees. Where are the trained bees?' He turned to the next item.

'They are doing a last-minute rehearsal just there, maestro.'

Suddenly they all heard a shout.

'Arrghhh! This bee is hovering too close. Gerroff me. Shoo!' shouted the female actor playing Shakuntala.

The actor playing Dushyanta started reciting sonorously,

'As the bee about her flies,
Swiftly her bewitching eyes
Turn to watch his flight;
She is practising today
Coquetry and glances-play,
Not from love but from fright –
Eager bee, you lightly skim
Over the eyelid's trembling rim
Towards the cheek aquiver,
Gently buzzing round her cheek,
Whispering in her ear you seek
Secrets to deliver,
While her hands that way and this
Strike at you, you steal a kiss…'

'Save me, someone save me!' shrieked the actor who was playing Shakuntala.

Kalidasa jumped in helpfully. 'No! No! There are still two lines before you are supposed to say that.'

She shrieked louder. 'I mean, ACTUALLY save me from this darned bee. It will kill me.' She ran off towards the fountain in the middle of the garden, trying to distract the bee.

'Maestro! The idea is symbolism! Can't the audience just *imagine* the bee?' The secretary was reaching the end of his tether.

'Everything must be perfect,' insisted Kalidasa mulishly. 'No straw elephants and such nonsense for MY play.'

'Well, how much can we train a bee?' The attendant looked like he was about to weep.

Noor shook her head in reluctant respect. Shri Kalidasa was quite as stubborn as she could be! She wandered off to the other side of the stage.

A strong odour suddenly hit her nose.

Ew. She peered down the side of the stage…at a huge dead fish, just lying there in a basket. Its dead eye glinted up at her glassily. Its middle was split open.

One of the attendants saw her look of horror and smirked. 'Oh, that's the fish that the ring is found in. Of course, Shri Kalidasa insisted there must be a *real* fish…and a *real* ring that is taken out of it and shown to the audience.'

A crazy idea occurred to Noor. She went and whispered urgently to the others, 'Guys! I got an idea what to do about our ring...'

'Perfect, Noor! I hate to say it, but you're not just a genius, you're ingenious!' Ansh cracked up at his own bad joke. Noor and Zoya rolled their eyes, while Rohan grinned.

Rohan volunteered to execute The Plan. He surreptitiously patted the ring, which was tucked away in the pouch hanging at his waist. He sauntered over to the dead fish, looking here and there nonchalantly. The others followed him one by one. When they had formed a sort of human curtain, Rohan turned and started poking around inside the dead fish.

'Yeurgh.' Noor shuddered involuntarily. Rohan finally managed to get the prop ring out of the dead fish and started to fumble inside his pouch for the massive diamond ring.

Plop. It fell from his hands to the ground. It lay there, its humongous diamond gleaming brightly in the sunlight.

'Well, well, well...what is going on here?' asked a deep baritone voice.

Uh-oh! They were done for.

• • • • • • • • • • • • • • •

They looked up and saw a very richly dressed man looking around.

Not at them. *Phew*.

Rohan quickly stepped on the ring with his bare foot to try and hide it. *Oooouch*. He felt the yell building up as the massive ring poked into the tender flesh but bit his lip hard to contain it.

The secretary came rushing up. 'Good afternoon, sire.' he said fawningly.

He turned to the children impatiently. 'Go on, pay your respects. This is the great *shreshthi*, Shri Anathapindika, whose house we are in.'

They all bowed their heads and said *pranam*. The secretary rebuked them. 'Well, what are you loitering around here for? Off with you.'

'No, we were just going to get the flowers,' said Zoya in as innocent a tone as she could manage.

'Well, be quick then,' he said, waiting.

Rohan said, 'Yesh-yesh, y'go, I'll jusht check 'n Elfu 'nd come.' He barely got the words out of his gritted teeth. He wiggled his eyebrows slightly.

Zoya caught on. 'Yes, okay, come soon.'

Thankfully, the secretary led the *shreshthi* off, and Rohan quickly picked up the ring and stuffed it inside the fish in one movement before hurrying off.

'I smell like fish...AND my foot hurts so badly!' groaned Rohan, limping up to the other three, who were waiting a little distance away.

'Yeah, you can change your name to...Reeky Ro,' said Noor, turning her nose up and laughing. She was just so happy she had not been the one to have to do this horrible poking around inside a fish.

Urgh! Rohan tried rinsing his hands as he passed by the fountain but stopped when he saw an attendant glaring at him from a distance.

'Guys, let's go in here and have a chat,' said Zoya. They turned into what was a small courtyard leading to a suite of rooms. They went into the closest room.

'Hmm...it looks empty,' said Noor. 'Look, Rohan, some sort of scent. Please apply liberally.'

'Look, we have put the ring where it will hopefully be discovered without us getting involved,' whispered Rohan, taking some scented ointment-thing and rubbing it all over his hands. Great. Now he smelt like a fishy rose. Or a rosy fish.

Zoya said urgently, 'Let's find King Vik, grab a hair, and get out. Soon! It's getting too complicated.'

'But we have to tell Vik that someone is out to kill him,' said Ansh in a panic. We can't just let them "off" him... and we can't be the ones who change the course of history if they do! Butterfly effect, remember?'

'And how precisely do you suggest we do that without ending up crushed into human-*bharta* under an elephant?' scoffed Noor.

As they were squabbling, they heard a loud squawk. And an overpowering scent.

Startled, they looked up...and their mouths fell open.

'Well, hello, young ones...and what are you doing in my private quarters?' asked a suave voice.

They looked up. A clean-shaven young man of about 19 or 20 stood there, smiling faintly at them and chewing something nonchalantly, a bright green parrot on his shoulder. He was a vision to behold. He was dressed in a sharply ironed, elaborate, yellow silk dhoti and *uttariya*, not a crease out of place. He had patterns drawn on his arms, and a fancy red tilak design on his forehead. His lips seemed to be rather red. He had gold jewellery everywhere on his body, a flower garland around his neck and a fancily carved walking stick in one hand.

'Wait, is that kajal in his eyes?' Noor asked Zoya, as softly as she could.

'Uh-hunh...and some sort of stain on his lips too,' Zoya whispered back from the side of her mouth.

'Wow, what is this scent?' Ansh asked faintly with a slight gagging motion. Noor rolled her eyes. 'Ansh! You gotta be less sensitive to smells, dude! Every. Single. Time!'

The youth stopped chewing and started pondering. 'Hmm, well, let's see. It could be my fragrant cream. Or my camphorated powder. Or the incense that perfumes my clothes. Or the flowers. Or my natural body scent.' He laughed.

Everyone's eyes grew rounder and rounder.

Ansh half-whispered, half-asked, 'And where is all of your hair?'

The young man replied sneeringly, 'Are you joking?' – pointing to his head. His head was a vision. Long, dark, lustrous hair tumbled down below his shoulder. The top half was done up in an elaborate bun. Pearls and flowers were wound through the hair. In fact, the hairdo looked like it should have its own name.

'Err, your body hair?' Ansh couldn't resist pushing it. They all looked. He didn't have a single hair on his body as far as they could make out.

'Oh, we pluck it all out…we're not savages after all,' the young man drawled, looking at his nails admiringly and slowly chewing whatever aromatic mixture he had in his mouth.

Rohan and Ansh looked at each other in horror. *Pluck out. All the body hair. One by one? Sheer torture!*

'Excuse me, sir, who are you?' ventured Zoya.

He looked at them. 'I should be asking you that, young ones…considering YOU are in MY private quarters. But…okay…I am Vishakhadutta. I am the only son of *shreshthi* Anathapindika, THE *nagaraka* of this city. And therefore, of ALL OF BHARATVARSHA. Any doubts?' He smirked.

There was a flurry as someone came into the room. It was the *shreshthi* they had encountered earlier. The scary one.

He asked thunderously, 'Where have you been? The guests are arriving. And where were you today, young man? I was waiting at the guild office all day.'

Vishakhadutta seemed quite unmoved. He gave a sweet smile. 'Daddy! I discovered this wonderful new wine at lunch today...from the south of Greece. Unbeatable. Much better than the Roman nonsense we've been having all this while. You must try it. So, the afternoon went in trying to track down the rest of the amphorae before they were sold off...'

'Daddy will become Dead-y if you keep this up, son! Why didn't you come in the morning?' grumbled the *shreshthi*.

'Wow, bad jokes are not just from our times,' whispered Ansh with a grin.

'Oh, come on! You know I have to be carried for my bath to the riverside, get a massage, do my workout, bathe properly. And this,' he pointed to himself, 'takes effort you know. I don't just wake up like this every morning.'

His father muttered something under his breath, which sounded suspiciously like, 'Why me, O Vishnu, why me? What sins did I commit in my past life to be punished like this?'

He said, slowly, with forced patience, 'Son, our business position has to be maintained. With hard work. That I do. Every day. Money doesn't grow on trees.'

'Ha! Ha!' Noor sniggered softly. 'My dad says that to me ALL THE TIME.'

Vishakhadutta continued obliviously. 'Yes, Daddy! Wait, look what I won from Gautamadutta today at gambling…this brilliant new parrot. Come, *mithu*, say what I taught you just now…'

The parrot looked here and there and squawked in Sanskrit, '*Pituh maam trahi.*'

Noor choked. Ansh giggled.

Rohan asked, 'Did that parrot just say…'

Zoya said, 'Save me from Daddy? Uh, yes…'

Vishakhadutta scolded the parrot. 'No, no, not that, little *mithu*! The other thing!' He looked at his father and shrugged sheepishly. 'A little more training perhaps…'

The *shreshthi* stood up, quivering in outrage. 'All this gambling-shambling has to stop. From tomorrow, start your work seriously or your allowance will be completely cut off.' He walked off in a huff.

Unfazed, Vishakhadutta turned to the children with a smile. 'Yes, where were we? Better go out, I s'pose.'

They kept looking at him awestruck. What a character!

•••••••••••••••

As they walked back to the garden, the sound of emphatic drumming started booming, cutting across the loud hum of the gathering. The noise of the party gradually faded away to an expectant silence.

A male voice announced loudly, 'Attention! Attention! Here comes his most illustrious majesty...the God-King! The Divinely Handsome! The Undefeated Warrior! The Incomparable! The Conqueror of Conquerors! The Emperor of Emperors...'

Ansh whispered, waggling his eyebrows, 'Not to mention the Humblest of Humbles...' Noor poked his side with her elbow to shush him, with a little giggle.

'...the dutiful son of the Bhattaraka Maharaja Rajadhiraja Samudragupta, and...the Ultimate Devotee of Vishnu...Maharajadhiraja Chandragupta Vikramaditya. Along with his Queen Consort, the most beauteous across the three worlds, the Ultimate Devotee of her husband, the Most Gracious, Maharani Dhruvaswamini...'

'Which three worlds?' wondered Ansh. Zoya gave him a sideways look and muttered, 'Err, the *trilok*? Heaven, Earth and the Underworld??'

Everyone turned to look as a large procession entered the vast garden. First came the royal couple. They were surrounded by a cluster of armoured bodyguards – all of them tall, fair, muscular...and very female! And clearly not from India!

'Why do all kings seem to have female bodyguards in India?' mused Rohan. 'And that too foreign ones? Very strange.'

Behind them was a younger girl, a princess by the looks of it, followed by an assortment of assistants and attendants. She was dressed in a heavy silk dhoti and blouse, in a bright yellow print. She was simply laden with jewellery. And flowers. And face paint. And more jewellery.

'Wow!' whispered Noor. 'Can't tell where the accessories end and she begins.'

Zoya replied 'Looks a bit much, no...wonder who... ohmigod, guys! That's PG! From this morning!'

The others all turned incredulously. The bedraggled girl from this morning and this ancient Indian statue lookalike? Zoya was right! They saw Prabhavati trying to walk demurely but shifting to a hop, skip and jump every few steps. A glare from a richly dressed lady walking by her side would settle her down...but just for a few moments!

Ansh said with a smirk. 'That lady looks like an older version of PG...must be her mum...only mums can get that specific expression of annoyance and pride just so!' He was so happy to be in the past – for once – rather than in a bathtub full of worms!

As the retinue came to a halt in front of the stage, the court poet was still droning sonorously, 'Just a few words

for our great emperor…He, on whose arm fame was inscribed by the sword…he, whose military genius still perfumes the oceans of the southern Deccan…he, who has attained sole supreme sovereignty over the entire world…he, the beauty of whose countenance is like the beauty of a full moon…'

The emperor smiled and made a gesture for him to stop. He said in a low timbred voice, 'Enough, enough. You mustn't praise me so much.'

The children just stood there, trying to absorb the image in front of them.

Emperor Vikramaditya was clearly a man at his physical peak! He was tall, with broad shoulders tapering into a tiny waist. Like everyone else, he wore a printed silk dhoti in a deep yellow, but his shone and gleamed in the sunlight. He had a luxuriant moustache, but no beard. His strong features curved into a slight, gracious smile as he looked over the gathering. He was simply dripping in gold. Heavy gold necklace like a collar, super-large earrings, arm- and wristbands, a belt – or was that two? – and even a gold tiara sort of thing resting on his blue turban. He also had a small flower crown on his head, and a flower garland.

Rohan gawked at his physique enviously. 'This guy is rrripped! Look at how broad that chest is.'

Ansh replied, 'Look at those abs, dude…is that an eight-pack? Do they even have gyms and weight machines here?'

Rohan said, 'And that hair…' They stared at the riot of dark curls tumbling down his shoulders.

Zoya had overheard and burst out laughing. Rolling her eyes, she said, 'Ansh! Ancient conquerors like him get fit by actually…fighting and running and riding…not just by going to the gym like modern people! See! Look at all those battle scars.' As they peered, they could see that his chest, arms and shoulders were mottled all over with scars…small and big! This seasoned warrior looked ready to fight in a micro-millisecond. And by the looks of it, crush his opponent too!

Noor poked Zoya. 'Look at the queen!'

Dhruvaswamini had an impossibly curvy hourglass figure, her waist nipping into almost unbelievably narrow dimensions. Her eyes were large and doe-like, expertly done up with kohl. Her lips were round and full, and her neck long and slender. And it seemed to be balancing a lot of weight, given how heavy her jewellery looked!

Noor exclaimed, 'Her earrings look like they need a person each to lift them…and that *maang-tika*! OMG.' She was now feeling quite pleased that they only had flower jewellery on.

Zoya said, 'But that hair!' Dhruvaswamini's hair was also like Chandragupta's…wildly curly, though hers was done up in an elaborate half updo.

A nearby courtier had heard her and spoke. 'Yes, like the rest of her, her hair is perfect too! Ideal hair…like an angry swarm of bees.'

'WAIT, WHAT? Hair like A.Swarm.Of.Bees?!' Noor caught the giggles. She doubled up, trying – unsuccessfully –

to stop laughing. 'Don't the two swarms of bees get tangled up with each other?' she choked out.

The courtier looked really offended. 'Who are you that you don't even know the ideal beauty when she is in front of you…our own exquisite Dhruvadevi… You can't be from here. Where are you from?!'

Uh-oh. Noor flushed bright red.

They quickly gave the same spiel as they had a few times before. 'We have been hired to help with the staging of venerated Shri Kalidasa's new play. We were just heading back to the…' Thankfully, the courtier lost interest and waved them away.

As they sidled back towards the stage, Prabhavati caught sight of Noor and started gesturing to catch her attention with a wide smile on her face.

'Welcome, everyone!' The *shreshthi* had come up on the stage.

•••••••••••••••

The *shreshthi* began speaking. 'It is a great honour and privilege for me to host this spring festival gathering, as we all come together to celebrate not only Vasantotsav, marking the season for rebirth of all life on Earth, but also the matrimonial alliance of our beloved princess Prabhavati with the esteemed Vakataka prince Rudrasena. And to mark the occasion, we have the first ever performance of our illustrious playwright, the peerless gem of literature, Shri Kalidasa's new play, *Abhijnanashakuntalam*!

'But first, Maharajadhiraja, we humbly request you to grace us with a short veena performance.'

With a gracious nod, Emperor Chandragupta stood up and went on to the stage. He said in a low, smooth voice, 'The business of kings is war. It is unavoidable and it is our dharma. But this…this is true joy. Music, dance, theatre, art, sculpture. Paying homage to the gods by creating beautiful things. Enjoying these with friends and family. This is the essence of an ideal life.'

He sat down cross-legged on a small square stool. A veena was placed across his lap, with the elongated blub resting on his right knee. He said, 'We will play Raga Bhairava today.' He closed his eyes in concentration and

began playing a beautiful, intricate melody, his left hand flying effortlessly up and down the strings, his right hand plucking independently.

The children looked on with wide eyes. This ferocious battle veteran, who seemed to be feared by all the land, had suddenly transformed into a skilled musician. It was so…startling. The past always showed you something unexpected, that was for sure!

At the end of the recital, there was silence for a few seconds until the audience came out of their trance-like state.

Noor whispered to the others, 'He is such a gifted musician…and I don't even like this stuff!'

The *shreshthi* came back on stage and announced, 'I now call upon the princess and the *yuvaraj*, and their parents to come up for the solemn exchange of rings.'

Prabhavati came on to the stage, a little nervous, a little excited. Behind her were her father and her mother. Queen Dhruvaswamini waited where she was, not looking too happy to lose the spotlight.

Next on stage was a youth of about 15–16. He was lanky and pale, and looked rather sickly, although he was dressed in rich finery. 'OMG…the Vakataka prince,' whispered Noor. He was followed by his parents.

Chandragupta Vikramaditya said formally, folding his hands, 'Dear in-laws, as you know we look forward to this alliance and to giving you our daughter. As you also know, the priceless Syamantaka *mani* – which we were going to gift you as a token of our new, eternal bond – has been stolen from us. This is not an insult or a stunt. Please forgive us.' He looked like he was swallowing hot acid. He was not a man used to apologizing to anyone.

The Vakataka king replied, 'Dear in-law and *maharajadhiraja*, what is a mere jewel compared to a bond of a lifetime with you and the lovely princess Prabhavati! Do not dwell on it.' He too looked like he was swallowing the same acid. The loss of the priceless Syamantaka *mani* was a heavy one to bear. He had never even got to see it! He'd heard it had magical powers of healing for those who kept it on their body for long periods of time.

A priest came on stage and began the ceremony. As the chanting and rituals came to an end, Chandragupta took a ring with a huge emerald and taking the prince's hand, made him wear it.

'Uh, what is happening?' enquired Rohan.

'Err, I think the emperor is getting engaged to the Vakataka prince!' replied Noor with a smirk.

Zoya rolled her eyes. 'Err, clearly this is the custom from ancient times, but it's quite unexpected, I have to say.'

As the royals took their seat, the *shreshthi* came back on and boomed, 'And now for the play.'

• • • • • • • • • • • • • • •

Kalidasa came up on the stage bashfully. Thunderous acclaim greeted him.

The playwright put his hands together and started his speech saying, 'Words fail me…'

Someone next to the children sniggered to his neighbour 'Haha! Not a chance! He who can take 20 sentences to describe…beautifully, I'll admit…what most people do in one!'

Kalidasa continued, 'I am beyond honoured to be given the opportunity to showcase the first performance of my new play in front of such an exalted audience. As usual, I went back to our ancient epics. In this case, the 'Jaya Samhita'…the Mahabharata…written by the original father of all poets, Maharishi Ved Vyasa, and penned by none other than Ganesh-ji. The story I wanted to recreate this time was that of the mother of Bharata, the ancestor of us all…yes, none other than Queen Shakuntala, and her marriage to King Dushyanta.'

He bowed off stage, saying, 'And let me start off with a little tribute to our mighty and gracious emperor.'

Two teenage boy actors came on the stage.

The play started.

The first one said, 'A majestic presence, yet it inspires confidence. Nor is this remarkable in a king who is half a saint. For to him…

'The splendid palace serves as a hermitage;
His royal government, courageous, sage,
Adds daily to his merit; it is given
To him to win applause from choirs of heaven
Whose anthems to his glory rise and swell,
Proclaiming him a king, and saint as well.'

The second youth asked, 'My friend, is this King Dushyanta, friend of Indra?'

As the first actor replied 'yes', the second broke out:

'Nor is it wonderful that one whose arm
Might bolt a city gate, should keep from harm
The whole broad earth dark-belted by the sea;
For when the gods in heaven with demons fight,
Dushyanta's bow and Indra's weapon bright
Are their reliance for victory.'

Both youths then exclaimed, 'Victory, O King Dushyanta! All hail!'

The actors then went up to Emperor Vikramaditya and offered him some flowers, which he accepted with a gracious smile.

The children realized that all that praise for Dushyanta was actually aimed at Emperor Vikramaditya.

'My god! So, you have to really butter up the king ALL the time in court, haan!' said Noor wryly with a subtle eye roll. 'I guess that's court life,' replied Zoya.

'I'm glad we live in a democracy,' inserted Ansh. 'Buttering up my mom all the time as it is, where would I have time to do that for a king, haha!'

As the play progressed, the children kept following the cues of the stage director and helping out where necessary. They were on tenterhooks to see what would happen in what they had dubbed The Fish Scene.

The trained bee got a few laughs and many awed gasps.

As Shakuntala lamented that Dushyanta had forgotten about her, eyes teared up in the audience. Even Zoya began to feel a little misty-eyed, looking at the performers' pathos.

Finally, it was time for The Fish Scene.

The fisherman picked up the basket containing the dead fish and presented its huge slimy body to the audience. Everyone gasped, and many wrinkled their noses as the strong, stale odour wafted across to them.

The basket was shown to the actor playing King Dushyanta, who asked – while peering closely at the fish – as tenderly as he could manage over the horrific smell, 'O Ring, why did you abandon that beautiful, delicate finger and fall in the water?'

King Dushyanta grimaced as he groped for the ring inside the slimy fish, and then tried to cover up his grimace with a weird half-smile. He lifted the ring out with a flourish and displayed it to the audience.

A loud exclamation echoed around the gathering as he held up the most gigantic ring with an oblivious smile.

Elfu was thrilled to see the ring he had kept for Madhumati! In a flash he plucked it out of the unsuspecting actor's hand and held it up in the tip of his trunk, admiring its glinting brilliance as he moved it.

Chandragupta Vikramaditya looked stunned. 'Why, that is the…' He turned to his attendant who nodded dumbly. Queen Dhruvadevi said breathlessly, 'That is the Syamantaka *mani*. I saw it just this morning!'

Pandemonium broke out.

'But how did it get inside the fish?'

'Who stole it? Who returned it?'

'This is unbelievable!'

The *shreshthi* came up and shouted for silence. 'O King, I want to say something. I think I saw *him* put it inside…' He pointed straight at Rohan!

Rohan's heart skipped a beat. He was in for it now. Within seconds, guards surrounded him and brought him close to the king.

'No, Your Maje-es-sty,' he stuttered 'You don't understand…'

The king looked very, very dangerous. And very, very threatening.

Prabhavati came forward. 'Please, you must listen to them, Father. They helped me.'

'You!' he thundered. 'How do you even know them?!'

Zoya had rushed forward with an anxious look. 'Your Exalted Majesty, please just hear us out.'

He raised his hand to gesture her to speak. 'Your Majesty, our elephant found this ring...and we think it was from the Shaka warrior.'

Chaos broke out again. 'Serious accusations!'... 'What Shakas?!'...'They are always plotting'... 'How can we even trust her?'

Zoya continued, trembling with the last of her courage, 'Your Majesty, we later overheard them...they want to kill you...and there is one of them!' She pointed to the far end of the stage where an extra was standing, dressed in tree bark like an ascetic.

The man stepped forward slowly and said, 'Well, if all else fails, this won't!' With a scream, the Shaka warrior, clenching a sharp dagger outstretched in his hand, began to run across the stage.

Straight towards Emperor Chandragupta Vikramaditya.

• • • • • • • • • • • • • • •

Chandragupta had wandered onto the stage and his female bodyguards were at a slight distance. Dressed in his party finery, he had neither arms nor armour.

Everyone was still and silent. It seemed like time had slowed down, waiting for the inevitable.

The assassin leapt towards the emperor, who had immediately crouched into a defensive stance, and then *whoosh*! One second he was there, and the next, the Shaka warrior had vanished.

Suddenly, there was a shout of 'Let me goooo!' Rohan realized the Elfu had plucked the Shaka off the floor, wrapped his trunk around his waist and was holding him up as if he was a log of wood, shaking his head slightly from side to side. The dagger went flying aimlessly through the air. Elfu ignored the man's flailing about, looking first at the king and then at Rohan, who had come rushing up.

Elfu didn't like this human. *Why is he screeching and shouting? Shush!* Hmm, Ro is making 'Down' gestures with his hands. *Why so frantic?* As his human brother's gesticulations increased in urgency, he decided sulkily, *Okay, fine. No one lets me do what I want, anyway.* Elfu shook his head strongly once, and abruptly straightened

his trunk. The man landed on the stage with a loud thud, and lay there for a second, winded.

When he opened his eyes, he was surrounded by the points of spears on all sides, held prisoner by the emperor's bodyguards. The game was up.

The emperor looked at his attendant, who immediately handed him his sword. Much more comfortable now that he was armed, he walked over to the would-be killer and growled, 'So, the Shakas have stooped so low now? I should kill you like the snake you are, right now!'

The bodyguards moved back slightly as the royal raised his sword menacingly. The Shaka lay there, in acceptance of his fate. He had tried. And failed. It was over now.

The children had been looking on with their hearts in their mouths. At Chandragupta's savage expression, they gasped as he brought his arm down. Ansh shut his eyes… he couldn't bear to look. *Silence?* He opened them gingerly and saw that the emperor had swerved away at the last second and was glaring at the man on the ground.

Somebody shouted from the audience. 'Wait! Isn't he the one who saved Yuvraj Kumaragupta from being trampled by an elephant today?'

King Chandragupta turned, thunderstruck. 'What?!'

As the story was hesitantly recounted by a tremulous Prabhavati, his face grew more and more thunderous. 'I will deal with you later, *rajkumari*,' he muttered threateningly.

He turned to the man on the ground and declared, 'I spare your life for this favour you did me today. Go! Go and tell your king that I will come and crush him soon. He'd better start preparing.'

He turned and walked off the stage, as the bodyguards forced the Shaka up and led him away, his hands bound roughly behind his back.

Dhruvaswamini came up to the emperor, trembling all over. She said tearfully, 'Swami…these Shakas will never leave me alone…I can't bear it…save me…SAVE ME!' She fell in his arms, swooning. He held her tenderly, stroking her hair comfortingly. 'I will always save you, Devi…'

All the people were still mostly frozen in place, shell-shocked by what had just happened.

Kalidasa, who was standing next to the children said, 'Now what is *that* about?!'

His neighbour said incredulously, 'Shri Kalidasa! Don't you know the story?! Oh, yes! You were in your *vanavaas* phase at that time, not willing to join the court…'

Zoya's ears perked up. *Ancient gossip! There was nothing she loved more.*

The neighbour continued in a whisper, 'You know that seven years ago, our most illustrious Samudragupta wanted his younger son, the most beloved emperor, to succeed him after his death. But Ramagupta, the older son, had the biggest fit over it! Said this is what the *shastras* say and whatnot. Anyway, you know our emperor has a big heart. He gave way out of duty to his elder brother.'

'Oh, really! Some muffled rumours had reached Ujjain, but they were squashed quite soon. So then what happened?' Kalidasa was intrigued.

'So then, Ramagupta was crowned emperor. He went on a tour of the empire, and the Shakas attacked. His camp was properly surrounded. He had no way out.

And in return for peace, that despicable Shaka king, that scoundrel, do you know what he wanted??'

'What? What?' Zoya stopped looking uninterested and turned her head to look openly at the narrator.

'It was...Ramagupta's wife...who happened to be... Dhruvaswamini Devi herself.'

'No!'

'Yes! And...Emperor Ramagupta agreed...'

'NO!'

'Uh-hunh. Yuvraj Chandragupta was also there. He could not bear this cowardly act...it made his blood boil. Do you know what he did?'

'What, what?' came a small chorus.

The courtier, happy to have found an audience, continued a little self-importantly, 'Our beloved emperor came up with the most audacious plan...the most courageous plan...the boldest plan...'

'Yes, yes, we get it, it was the best-est plan in the history of plans...please continue!' said Kalidasa, a little testily.

'Yes, well, so Yuvraj Chandragupta decided to dress up as Dhruvadevi and a few soldiers dressed up as her "attendants", all heavily veiled, of course. They went up to surrender themselves in a row of palanquins.'

Kalidasa's expression was unconvinced. 'Wait a minute! Are you trying to tell me that a group of hulking warriors were convincing as our dainty queen Dhruvadevi and her delicate handmaidens?'

The courtier looked a bit annoyed. 'Yes, well, they pulled it off! There is nothing our emperor can't do! Are you interested in the rest...or...?'

'No, no, please go on!'

'So, once inside the camp, they threw off their veils and launched a ferocious attack on the Shakas. They were heavily outnumbered, but did that stop them?! NO! He killed that rascal Shaka king and came back victorious.'

'And then?' They were all hanging on to every word.

'Well…as you can imagine, this didn't sit too well with Ramagupta. Completely outclassed by his own younger brother. Hero of the Gupta forces! Anyway, they all went to bed…and at night…someone attacked Yuvaraj Chandragupta. He sleeps with his sword next to him, so he killed the attacker in the dark.

'And when the lamps were lit in the tent, guess who it turned out to be?'

'Noooooo way! Are you serious…Ramag…' Zoya jumped in, unable to help herself.

'Yes, young lady…unable to bear the humiliation, Ramagupta himself had attacked our heroic emperor and paid the ultimate price for it.' The courtier smiled ghoulishly.

'Well, the next day, we courtiers were so pleased to crown our beloved emperor Chandragupta to his rightful throne. In fact, we insisted that he marry the graceful lady of unparalleled loveliness across the three worlds, Dhruvaswamini Devi…

'So yes, this the story of how Chandragupta came to be the mighty emperor and Dhruvadevi his chief maharani.'

'What drama, what a climax…someone should write a play about this,' said Kalidasa, shaking his head admiringly.

• • • • • • • • • • • • • • • •

The emperor had returned to the stage and his attendant clapped his hands loudly. 'Attention, everyone!'

All the guests turned towards the stage.

The emperor said, 'Well, I am sure I speak for everyone when I say this has been a dramatic turn of events. No less than a play! But all's well that ends well.' He laughed with some relief. The danger had been very real.

'I would like to present this magical and priceless Syamantaka *mani* to the esteemed Vakatakas and so seal our alliance forever.' The young prince Rudrasena came onstage again and Chandragupta placed the ring on his other finger. It covered most of his thin hand, which suddenly dropped under the weight.

The king wasn't done yet. 'I would also like to give a token of my appreciation to these brave children who have definitely saved the day, and most likely my life.'

He held out thick gold earrings with intricate filigree work. Zoya went up to him hesitantly. As she reached forward to receive the earrings, she stumbled and bumped into Chandragupta with some force. Immediately his ferocious female bodyguards surrounded her. 'Back down,' he said to them, smiling as he righted Zoya. She clutched her hands…hiding the hair she had managed to pluck out.

As she backed away and reached her friends she whispered in English. 'My phone is beeping. Let's go.' They began backing away from the scene.

'WAIT!' boomed the emperor's voice.

Uh. They stopped, frozen in their tracks. Now what?

Chandragupta smiled brilliantly. 'And for this brave little elephant, here is something for you too'. He was handed something by his attendant, which he held out with a flourish. The children looked on in awe. It was a gold coin. Elfu sniffed around the emperor's palm, before picking it up delicately and folding it into his long trunk. *Shiny! Maybe he could present it to Madhumati…whenever he saw her next.*

His daydream was rudely interrupted as Rohan gently plucked the gold coin from his trunk and handed it to Zoya.

Prabhavati smiled slightly and waved subtly at them. They gestured back with waves and big smiles.

It was time to leave.

'Let's go, Elfu! Too many assassins and dead fish and other hazards here.' Rohan tugged on his trunk lightly.

Elfu was NOT happy with this plan. *What about Honey, he meant Madhu-ji…he wanted to spend more time with her!*

They reached the elephant parking lot, and went beyond it, Zoya's phone indicating the way. As they approached the riverside, they saw a life-size statue of a lady.

Noor exclaimed, 'OMG! This looks exactly like that queen we just saw!'

Ansh chimed in helpfully, 'Queen Dhruvaswamini…'

Zoya got her explaining look on. 'Guys, this is a statue of a *yakshini*. They were demi-godd…'

Noor interrupted, 'Yes, yes – Zoya, look she has a star on the belt. I think this is how we get back…let's goooo …'

'Come on people, let's do it!' whispered Rohan.

And with a press of the button and a whoosh they were off, spinning crazily in the darkness until the world had stilled.

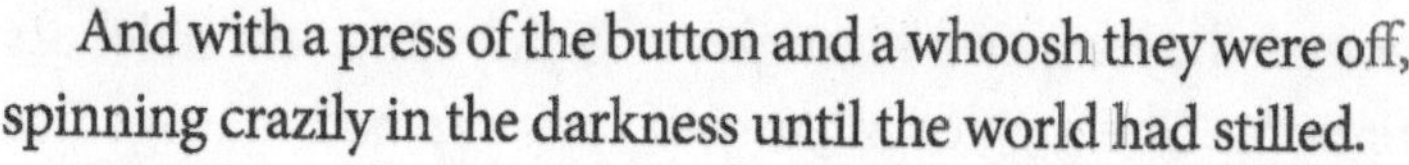

They were back at the cave-office. Sid Lal had been waiting anxiously. 'Well, did you get it?'

When she handed over the super-curly hair, he gave her a big smile. 'Well done, Ms Ali. And the rest of you. We are going to do great work together.'

Though she was pleased at the praise, Zoya noticed somewhere in her mind that this guy always asked for the hair first – even before checking whether they were okay after undertaking such a dangerous journey! Hmm.

They decided to walk back instead of using the Hyperloop again.

'Man, that was cray-cray!'

'Always more than you expect, huh?'

'Elfu, you really saved the day, buddy,' said Rohan, rubbing his elephant brother's trunk fondly.

Finally, narrowly escaping Nirvana Aunty's attention, the children made it back to their own houses.

Zoya was back in her room. She took out the small wooden chest from under her bed and unlocked it. Oh man! She reached into her pouch, pulling out a few strands of dark brown hair. Now which hair was Chandragupta's, and which one was Kalidasa's? Something had urged her not to tell Sid Lal about this. She stared at the two strands of hair with a perplexed frown. Oh, wait…duh! She looked and saw which one was more tightly curled. She thought about the emperor's tangle of wild curls. Bumblebees fighting. She giggled silently. If only she had managed to get a hair off Aryabhata. Sigh.

Zoya labelled each carefully, before storing them in the chest where she was secretly collecting the treasures from their adventures.

She sat back on her bed with a satisfied sigh.

Would they be back?

What adventures were in store for them?

Who knew.

• • • • • • • • • • • • • • •

LIBERTIES WE HAVE TAKEN WITH THE FACTS

Aryabhata: *Chandragupta II Vikramaditya ruled from 376* CE *to 415* CE*. Aryabhata was born in 476* CE*, almost a hundred years later, according to the birthdate mentioned in the* Aryabhatiya, *his text on astronomy. We have taken the huge liberty of placing Aryabhata a hundred years before his time, because we wanted to showcase the Gupta period's science, astronomy and mathematics, which were among the most advanced in the world at the time.*

Kumaragupta: *We have based this book in 383* CE*, when Prabhavati Gupta would have been, say, 13 years old. Kumaragupta, Chandragupta Vikramaditya's successor, was born in 399* CE*. We have shown his birth nearly two decades in advance.*

Chandragupta playing the veena: *Chandragupta's father Samudragupta was known for his musical skills and is shown playing the veena on his gold coins. We have assumed that Chandragupta too would have known how to play the veena.*

Shaka assassination plot: *We do not know of any plot by the Shakas attempting to assassinate Chandragupta Vikramaditya.*

The diamond ring: *India was the only known source of diamonds in the world right until the 17th century. There are many tales about huge diamonds in Indian literature, including the Syamantaka* mani *owned by Lord Krishna.*

We have taken the description of the diamond in the ring from that of the Great Moghul diamond as described by the French traveller Jean Baptiste Tavernier. It had originally been presented at a weight of 787 carats to Mughal emperor Shah Jahan, from Golconda. It had been badly cut and reduced to 280 carats when Tavernier saw it. Looted by Nadir Shah and taken to Iran, it disappeared thereafter, though some claim that the famous Russian Orlov diamond is a mutilated version of it.

For such an important period in India's history, there are surprisingly very few written records available to us from this time. We have to rely heavily on inscriptions, coins, archaeological records and literature from the time. There is an uncertainty about dates and biographical details of even important figures like Chandragupta Vikramaditya, Prabhavati Gupta and Kalidasa.

FACT TRACKER

More About the Guptas

The Gupta Empire period is famously known as India's 'golden age' - the country was peaceful and prosperous, it had great international universities, and brilliant art and literature. At its peak, the Gupta Empire had more people (50 million!) and more wealth than its contemporaries, the Byzantine Roman and the Persian Sassanid Empires.

There was a burst of creativity in many fields, from the sciences, literature and sculpture to painting, dance, music and poetry. Indian science, metallurgy and mathematics became the most advanced in the world. The zero and decimal system were already in use. It was a period of intensive foreign trade and interaction, particularly with China and South-East Asia.

THE GUPTA EMPIRE

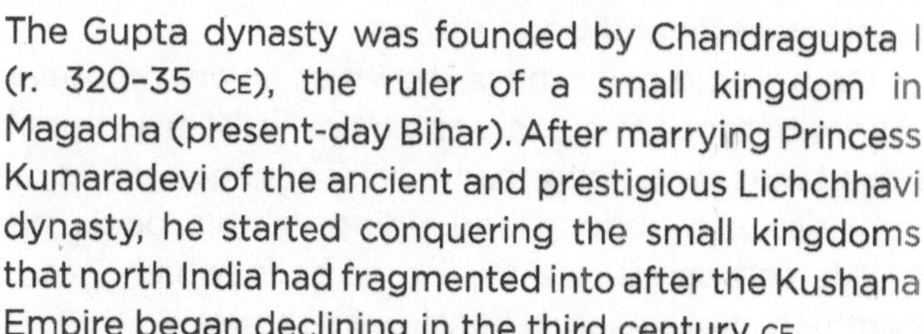

The Gupta dynasty was founded by Chandragupta I (r. 320–35 CE), the ruler of a small kingdom in Magadha (present-day Bihar). After marrying Princess Kumaradevi of the ancient and prestigious Lichchhavi dynasty, he started conquering the small kingdoms that north India had fragmented into after the Kushana Empire began declining in the third century CE.

His son, the magnificent Samudragupta, was called the 'Napoleon of India' by 19th century British historians.

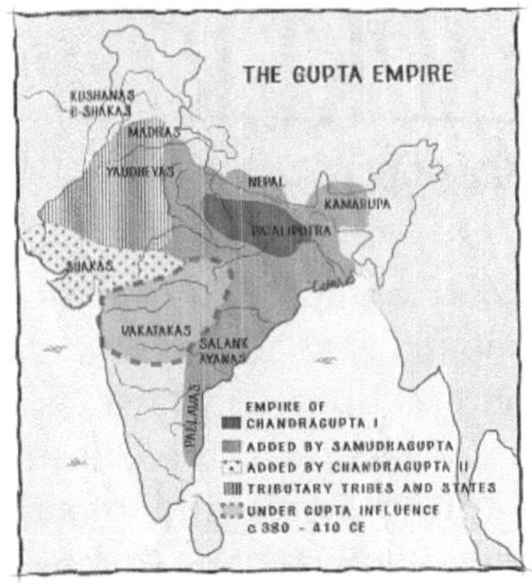

With his conquests, the Gupta Empire included today's Bihar, Bengal, Uttar Pradesh, Rajasthan and Punjab. A host of kingdoms from Gandhara in the north, the Shakas in Gujarat and Malwa, the Pallavas of Kanchipuram and Sri Lanka, and Assam and Nepal, all bowed before Samudragupta, whose favourite title became the tongue-twister Jayatyajitarajajetajitah, 'the unconquered conqueror of unconquered kings'! Samudragupta also maintained a significant navy, and international sea trade thrived.

◆ Chandragupta Vikramaditya ◆

Chandragupta II Vikramaditya, the son of Samudragupta, ruled for nearly 40 years, from c. 375 CE to 415 CE. His reign is considered the peak of the Gupta Empire. He further expanded the empire, notably defeating the Shakas who ruled in Gujarat and Rajasthan, and gaining access to profitable western ports and trade routes.

On his gold coins, he is shown as a very muscular man with broad shoulders and a tiny waist, a luxuriant moustache and long curly hair, engaged in royal activities like hunting and riding. In this book, his hair is compared to a swarm of bees, which was a common simile used in Sanskrit literature!

There is a famous play, *Devi Chandragupta,* by the sixth century CE playwright Vishakhadutta. It tells the following story. Upon Samudragupta's death, his elder son Ramagupta became king. He was defeated by the Shakas in western India, and pusillanimously agreed to surrender his wife, the beautiful Dhruvaswamini, to the enemy. His younger brother Chandragupta was furious, and disguised himself as the queen to ambush and kill the Shaka king. Soon, Chandragupta also killed his elder brother claiming 'self-defence', married Dhruvaswamini and crowned himself emperor. We don't really know if this is what happened, but in our book we have treated it as true.

Many of us are familiar with the seven-metre-tall Iron pillar in the Qutub complex, which is a marvel of metallurgy, as it has not rusted in 1,600 years! Probably installed by Chandragupta Vikramaditya, its Sanskrit inscription speaks of the mighty King Chandra, who had a countenance 'as beautiful as the full moon'. He crossed the 'seven rivers of the Sindhu' and conquered the north-west, and perfumed the southern seas by the breeze of his valour.

THE IRON PILLAR, DELHI

The Later Guptas

Chandragupta Vikramaditya was succeeded by Kumaragupta I (r. 415–55 CE), his son born to Dhruvadevi. Kumaragupta's prosperous 40-year reign is known for its flourishing art and culture.

However, by his reign, the Central Asian nomadic Huns had begun their brutal attacks on India, crossing the Hindu Kush mountains into the Gandhara region in the north-west of the Indian subcontinent. Kumaragupta's son Skandagupta (r. 455–67 CE) spent most of his time battling them. Under the sustained Hun onslaught, by 510 CE, the Gupta Empire had mostly crumbled, and minor branches of the family broke away to become independent rulers of small kingdoms.

Prabhavati Gupta

One of the earliest women rulers that we know of in India is Prabhavati Gupta (probably born around 370 CE), the daughter of Chandragupta Vikramaditya and his wife Kuberanaga, a Naga dynasty princess.

Prabhavati was married to the Vakataka king Rudrasena II. The Vakatakas (c. 250–500 CE) ruled much of present-day Maharashtra, and it was during their reign that most of the Ajanta cave paintings near Aurangabad were created.

The alliance with the Vakatakas would have been important for Chandragupta as a common front against the Shaka rulers, which is a focus in the book.

Rudrasena II died soon after the wedding, leaving behind three young sons. Prabhavati Gupta ruled as regent for 20 years (390–410 CE) until her son Pravarsena became the ruler. Though we glean some information about her from inscriptions, we know nothing about her personality or looks.

The earliest mention of the name Maharashtra is in a seventh-century inscription at Aihole by Chalukya king Pulakeshin II, proclaiming sovereignty over the 'three Maharashtrakas with their 99,000 villages'.

Governing the Empire

The Guptas ruled in a feudal style, with a hierarchy of nobles reporting to the king. Conquered kings were not displaced, but became subsidiary rulers.

According to the Chinese Buddhist pilgrim Faxian, the people were well off, lightly taxed and free to move throughout the empire. Punishment was lenient, and the death penalty rare. Monetary fines, based on the severity of the crime, were the common method of justice.

Gupta Coins

As the Guptas grew rich, they started minting gold coins in India - these were called Dinars and portrayed the governing king on one side, while the reverse depicted goddesses like Lakshmi. They were beautiful works of art depicting the emperor hunting, playing the veena or in thoughtful repose.

COIN OF SAMUDRAGUPTA SHOWS HIM PLAYING THE VEENA

Religion

The Guptas worshipped Krishna and called themselves Parama Bhagavata, Vasudev Krishna's 'ultimate devotees'. Their royal emblem was the Garuda, Vishnu's divine mount. The period saw a great resurgence of Hinduism after the dominance of Buddhism during the preceding two empires, the Mauryan and the Kushana.

The Guptas conducted Vedic yagnas, including the prestigious Ashvamedha horse sacrifice.

Buddhism, though no longer at its peak, still flourished. The Chinese traveller Faxian, who visited India during the reign of Chandragupta Vikramaditya, speaks of a landscape dotted with thousands of stupas and monasteries. Gorgeous cave temples were hewn out of the mountainside, and Kumaragupta I founded the great Buddhist university of Nalanda (close to present-day Patna).

Jainism was also popular, especially in the Karnataka region. In many places like Ellora, Aihole and Badami, Buddhist caves, Jain shrines and Hindu temples are all located together, with very similar architecture.

RUINS OF NALANDA UNIVERSITY

Trade and Economy

Trade flourished, with Indian and foreign merchants travelling all over the vast empire, seeking fine fabrics, rare gems and spices. The Silk Route connecting the East to Europe was still important, allowing Indians to connect with it in Central Asia. Kalyan, Malabar, Mangaluru and Tamralipti were key port cities for trade with the Byzantine Romans in the West, and South-East Asia, Sri Lanka and China in the East.

ANATHAPINDIKA SUPPOSEDLY HAD THE ENTIRE JETVANA PAVED WITH COINS, BHARHUT

Some merchants were very rich. Anathapindika was a merchant from Shravasti who, from Buddhist sources, is known to have gifted the Buddha an enormous tract of land called Jetvana. (We have used his name to denote a very rich *shreshthi* in Pataliputra. Buddhist literature mentions idle, fashionable sons of rich merchants (we have modelled the hard-working *shreshthi*'s indolent, foppish son Vishakhadutta on them, and given him the name of a later Gupta playwright.)

Women and Men

In the Gupta period writings, descriptions of ideal female beauty feature interesting comparisons with natural objects and creatures: eyes like a deer, skin as brilliant as a dark blue lotus, or light as gold, teeth like pearls, and a walk like an elephant!

Women from wealthy households were educated. There were 64 *kala*s or skills, which were supposed to be acquired by elite men and women. Some of the more unusual ones of these were: arraying beds or couches with flowers; colouring teeth, garments, hair, nails and bodies; binding of turbans; making topknots of flowers; magic or sorcery; solving riddles, enigmas and puzzles; teaching parrots and mynahs to speak; and disguising appearance!

The Arts

The Gupta period was called 'golden' for its gracious living, and beauty and symmetry in every aspect of life. As a poet of the time, Bhartrihari, wrote: *A man without knowledge of literature, music and art is veritably a beast without horns or tail.* Even kings moved beyond the business of building empires and delighted in their personal talents in writing, painting and music.

STANDING BUDDHA, C. FIFTH CENTURY CE

The age produced some of the world's finest art and sculpture, and images of Hindu, Jain and Buddhist deities were made in stone and terracotta across the country. The sculptures were initially produced at specialized centres such as Mathura, Gandhara and Sarnath, but gradually spread and influenced future generations inside and outside India, especially South-East Asia.

The few Gupta temples that survived the continuous waves of invasions include the Ajanta and Ellora caves (developed under Vakataka rule in the Gupta period), the Dashavatara Temple at Deogarh near Jhansi, and the Udayagiri caves near Bhopal. The terracotta-and-brick temple in Bhitargaon near Kanpur has India's earliest known vaulted arch.

BHITARGAON BRICK TEMPLE

Painting was also highly developed, though little remains for us to see, other than the sophisticated Ajanta frescoes. Literary sources tell us that temples and houses were richly decorated with wall paintings. A culture of portraiture existed, mentioned often in Kalidasa's works.

Literature and Language

Sanskrit once again came to the centre stage after centuries of neglect, and replaced Prakrit as the major language of scholarship, writing and even speech. Great libraries were created in universities such as Nalanda, and many foreign monks came to India to study there.

Poets and writers were very skilled with word play – the sounds of words, double meanings, similes, metaphors and allusions.

The Panchatantra's animal tales, still popular today, were translated as *Kalilah wa Dimnah* into Arabic and travelled to the West.

Theatre, Kalidas and Shakuntala

Kalidasa, considered among the greatest Sanskrit writers, embodied the spirit of his age. He describes the beauties of nature and of love exquisitely in his plays, such as *Malavikagnimitram* and *Abhijnanashakuntalam*. His poems like the *Meghadutam* and *Raghuvamsham* still influence modern Indian poetry. (We have taken actual excerpts from Shakuntala, though the trained bee is from our imagination! Also, we are reasonably confident that Kalidasa wouldn't have used real animals for his plays – ancient plays normally used fabric animals stuffed with straw.)

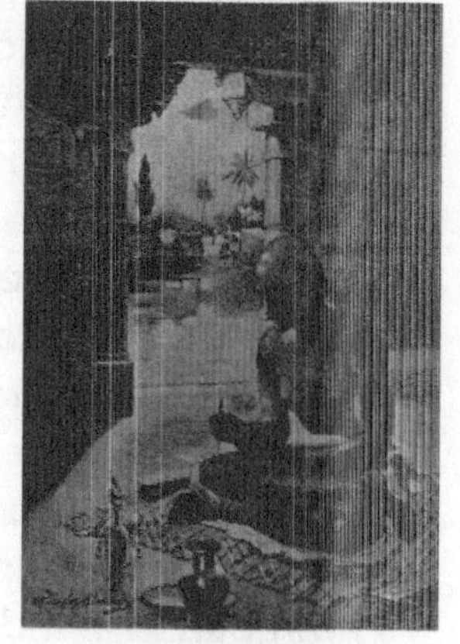

ARTIST'S IMPRESSION OF KALIDASA WRITING *MEGHADUTAM*

It was a peculiar feature of Sanskrit plays that the servants and women spoke in Prakrit languages, and only upper-caste men used Sanskrit - perhaps a sad reflection of how it really was.

The Guptas and the Rest of the World

Visitors, traders and students came from China, Korea and South-East Asia in the East, and Arabia, Persia and the Byzantine Roman empire in the West. Cosmas Indicopleustes, a Greek merchant from Alexandria, Egypt, left records of his travels in India in the sixth century CE.

Indians traded with a land called Suvarnabhumi in the East. Burma, Thailand and Indonesia today all lay claim to being that 'Land of Gold'. In fact, the airport in Bangkok is called the Suvarnabhumi Airport!

The tale of Gangaraja, the king of Champa - an ancient kingdom in southern Vietnam - who abdicated his throne and came to India to die in Kashi (now Varanasi in Uttar Pradesh), is mentioned in a Chinese text from the seventh century, *History of the Southern Dynasties.* All of South-East Asia adopted many aspects of Indian culture. They followed Hinduism and Buddhism, and used Sanskrit. (That's why we named the Vietnamese elephants Madhumati and Paramsundari. The king's attendant's name, Kandarpadharma, is also from an inscription.) There are still a small community of Hindu Cham people in southern Vietnam, called Balomons, from the word 'Brahmin'!

There is a large number of Hindu temple complexes across South-East Asia, of which the most famous are Angkor Wat in Cambodia, My Son in Vietnam and Prambanan in Indonesia.

Indian kings often had foreign women bodyguards called Yavanis, who were Greek or Central Asian in origin. (We have called Prabhavati Gupta's bodyguard Helena, a popular Greek name.)

Faxian was a Chinese Buddhist monk who visited India during Chandragupta Vikramaditya's reign, around 400 CE. He came by the land route over the Himalayas, and returned 17 years later by sea. He mentions that rich traders in Pataliputra had set up free hospitals for the poor. His descriptions of daily life are quite rosy, and can perhaps be taken with a pinch of salt as he probably wanted his 'holy land' to be perfect!

Fashion and Jewellery

The classic unstitched Indian garment set of *antariya* (lower garment - dhoti), *uttariya* (upper garment - like a scarf) and *kayabandha* (cummerbund) were worn by both men and women. The Ajanta illustrations show some women wearing stitched blouses along with the usual strapless look. Beautifully dyed, printed, woven and embroidered fabrics in cotton, silk and wool were used. We see *ikat*, *bandhani* and other classic Indian fabric patterns. Cotton muslins, so fine that they moved with every breath, were a speciality and much in demand overseas (Indian muslin was more expensive than Chinese silk in ancient Rome!).

People knotted their turbans in different ways for different occasions - one way for festivals, another for court visits and a third for visiting shops!

Jewellery, especially gold, remained very popular with both men and women. There were jewels for every conceivable (and inconceivable) part of the body - *chudamani* (hair ornaments), hair meshes, earrings, necklaces, rings, bracelets, belts and anklets. Pearls were very popular.

Hairstyling was an elaborate art. Men were normally clean-shaven, but many kept long hair. Intricate hairstyles combined braids, loops and knots for women, and were embellished with flowers, jewels, and nets of pearls. Ointments from plants were used as perfumes, particularly sandalwood. Hair was perfumed with agar smoke.

Body and face art were very popular, with tilak*s*, and floral patterns painted on the cheeks in different colours by specialists. We still see traces of this in the designs painted on the faces of Bengali brides! *Anjan* (kohl) was applied to the eyes, women coloured their lips with shellac, and used *paan* and the citron fruit (*bijapuraka*) to freshen their breath.

Flowers were an integral part of daily wear, and both men and women wore intricate garlands and floral jewellery.

HEAD OF PARVATI. SHOWING AN INTRICATE GUPTA-STYLE HAIRDO

Food

The main grains continued to be barley, wheat and rice. Sugar was refined in many ways, to make *gur*, *khand*, *shakkar* and other products. *Modak*s were very popular sweets. Milk and its products like butter, ghee and yoghurt remained important. (We have shown the children enjoying *shikharini*, a thick drink made with yoghurt, cardamom and imported cloves.) Meat, including deer, wild boar and fish were common, though Faxian talks of widespread vegetarianism.

◆ Science ◆

There was a great profusion of ideas, with traditional views of the cosmos – where the earth balanced on a serpent's head – coexisting with a round earth that rotated on its own axis!

Indian mathematics, astronomy and metallurgy were probably the most advanced in the world.

The Bakhshali manuscript from Kashmir records the first written use of the zero. The Romans were still using their clunky numeral system, and the largest number they had a name for was the Greek 'myriad', or 10,000! Using the decimal system, Indians had conceptualized vast numbers.

Aryabhata was a mathematician and astronomer from Ujjain, who spent many years in Pataliputra. He calculated the value of pi to the fourth decimal, created tables of the trigonometric sine function, and claimed that the earth was round and rotated on an axis. He accurately calculated the circumference of the earth and also correctly explained eclipses by saying that the moon came between the sun and the earth!

Varahamihira, the astronomer, summarized the five prevalent schools of astronomy in the *Panchasiddhantika*. His *Brihat-samhita* was a wide-ranging encyclopaedia, covering topics as varied as agriculture, marriage and gemstones.

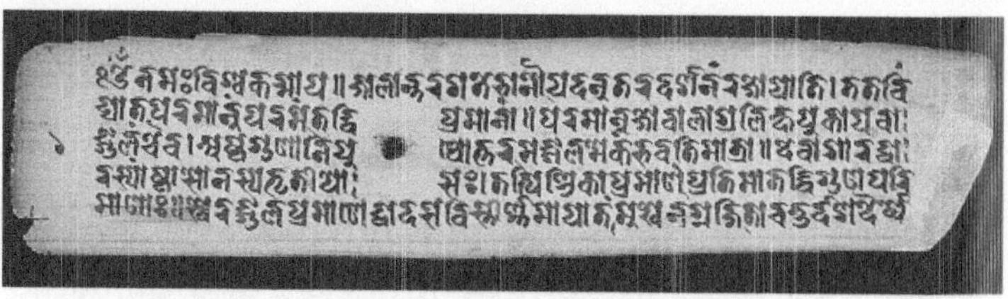

A LATER MANUSCRIPT OF VARAHAMIHIRA'S *BRIHAT-SAMHITA*

Another later important astronomer was Brahmagupta, whose texts introduced Indian astronomy to the Arabs. His text *Brahmasphuta-siddhanta* included early concepts of the earth's gravity: 'All heavy things are attracted towards the centre of the earth...all people on earth stand upright, and all heavy things fall down...by a law of nature.'

THE SHAKAS

The Scythians (Shakas) were horse-riding nomadic tribes, who spoke Indo-European languages and had been roaming the vast tracts of the Asian steppes for thousands of years. They have been mentioned by the Greeks, Persians and Romans since antiquity. Exceptional horsemen, they were renowned for their deadly aim with bows and arrows whilst in full gallop. They used ingeniously engineered composite bows, made by layering materials like horn, wood and sinew. Each bow could take up to two years to make.

Shaka women lived on a far more equal footing with men, fighting in wars, and often becoming rulers. The Greek myths about the Amazons, the tribe of fierce warrior women, are thought to have been inspired by Greek encounters with Scythian women warriors. (The horse and archery displays described in this book are taken from ancient descriptions of Scythian horsemanship.)

The Shakas in India

The Shakas came in from Central Asia and defeated the Indo-Greek rulers who had been ruling in Punjab since 200 years. The first Shaka king in India - Moga or Maues (50 BCE) - settled in Gandhara.

At the beginning of the first millennium, the Kushanas, another Indo-European tribe, came into India and defeated the Shakas. Many of these Shaka rulers became *kshatraps*, or feudal rulers, under the Kushanas, and began ruling as independent Western Kshatrap dynasties after Kushana power weakened.

COINS OF MAUES, FIRST SHAKA KING IN INDIA

Rudradamana (130–50 CE) was a prominent Shaka ruler. We know him through an inscription on a rock in Junagadh in Gujarat. This is the earliest Sanskrit inscription found anywhere in India – or the world!

At the time that this book is set in, Rudrasimha III was the Western Kshatrap ruler, ruling over present-day Gujarat, Rajasthan and parts of Madhya Pradesh. He was defeated decisively by Chandragupta Vikramaditya by 399 CE.

The Shakas assimilated into India, following Buddhism and Hinduism. Many were Shiva devotees in this period. (We have portrayed some of the tensions that must have existed between the Shakas, the Guptas and the Vakatakas. Virdaman and Ushavadata were actual Shaka names of that period.)

The Shakas of western India spoke the Shaka language, also known as Khotanese, as it was first identified in the region of Khotan, now in China.

Shaka men wore stitched clothes designed to facilitate riding horses: a long tunic, covered with a coat (*chugha*), and trousers - either close-fitting churidars or loose salwars. They sported full moustaches and wore padded boots. Headgear could be the Scythian pointed cap. The gorgeous scaled armours for men and horses described in the book are based on findings in Scythian graves.

THE GANGETIC DOLPHIN

The Ganges river dolphin (*Platanista gangetica*), India's National Aquatic Animal, lives in the Ganga and related rivers. It is known by the name *susu* and other similar sounding names in different Indian languages. In Indian mythology, the Ganges dolphin is associated with the river goddess Ganga and is occasionally the depiction of her *vahana*, the Makara.

Unlike the popular depictions of friendly, frolicking dolphins, male dolphins in the sea are known to often form little bully gangs, which we have depicted just for fun.

GODDESS GANGA ON A MAKARA

KASHMIR

Kashmir was a major university centre in ancient India. Sharada University was a particularly renowned centre for Buddhist studies. Many of the Buddhist monks who went to China were from Kashmir. Kashmir's history has been very well documented by Kalhana in his *Rajatarangini*. The children's names are derived from the names of the rulers of Kashmir from that period. Many of the male names ended in '-aditya', like the conquerer Lalitaditya, and female names ended in '-mati', like the queen Yashomati.

WHITE ELEPHANTS

White elephants are extremely rare, and would occur naturally, either as albinos, or otherwise. They were considered very special and sacred, and in Thailand, only the king was allowed to own white elephants. The 'white' elephant is not entirely white. Most are pale pink or light grey.

WORM SPA

Insects have been used all over the world since time immemorial for medicine and cosmetic therapy. Live leeches were used to bleed toxins from patients until quite recently. Live maggot therapy was used in America and Eurasia, and by aborigines in Australia to treat wounds. Many spas offer a fish pedicure, where live fish nibble away the dead skin from your feet. A worm spa does not exist yet...but who knows!

HYPERLOOP

A hyperloop is a high-speed transportation method proposed by Elon Musk in 2012 - imagining speeds of up to 1,000 kilometres per hour (km/h). There is a long, sealed tube at low pressure, in which a pod moves, using magnetic propulsion, between two terminals. Virgin Hyperloop conducted the first trial in 2020 in Las Vegas, USA, reaching a top speed of 172 km/h (a long way to go!). In India, hyperloop routes have been proposed between Chennai and Bengaluru (30 minutes), and Mumbai and Pune (20 minutes)! No hyperloops are operational anywhere in the world yet.

Page 114: Map by Syed Salahuddin from *The History of India for Children*, Vol I, Hachette India; **Page 115:** Iron Pillar: Wikimedia Commons Public Domain; **Page 117:** Gupta coin: Wikimedia Commons: Attribution: Classical Numismatic Group, Inc. http://www.cngcoins.com; under Creative Commons Attribution-Share Alike 3.0 Unported license; **Page 118: (middle)** Nalanda: Shutterstock; **(bottom)** Bharhut sculpture: Wikimedia Commons Public Domain; Author: Beglar, Joseph David, 1875; source: British Library; **Page 120: (top)** Standing Buddha: Government Open Data License - India; Copyright © 2017 The Presidents Secretariat, Rashtrapati Bhavan; https://commons.wikimedia.org/wiki/File:Rashtrapati_Bhavan_Buddha,_Mathura,_5th_century_(black_background).jpg; **(bottom)** Bhitargaon Temple: Wikimedia Commons Public Domain; Author: Beglar, Joseph David, 1875; source: British Library; **Page 121:** Kalidasa: Wikimedia Commons Public Domain; Author: W. Douglas; **Page 124:** Goddess Parvati head: by Mistunee Chowdhury; *The History of Idia for Children*, Vol. I, Hachette India; **Page 125:** Brihat-Samhita: Wikimedia Commons Creative Commons Attribution-Share Alike 4.0 International license; Author: Ms Sarah Welch; **Page 127:** Shaka coins: Attribution: Classical Numismatic Group, Inc. http://www.cngcoins.com; under Creative Commons Attribution-Share Alike 2.5 Generic license; **Page 128:** Goddess Ganga on the Makara: Wikimedia Commons Public Domain; Source: The Bodleian Libraries, Oxford University, UK; https://commons.wikimedia.org/wiki/File:Ganga_Kalighat_1875.jpg